Guerrilla Yardwork

The First-Time Home Owner's Handbook

I0087111

American
ROBOTNIK

Text, layout, cover image & design © 2013 Peter Korchnak
PeterKorchnak.com
Illustrations © 2013 Jen McClure
behance.net/JenMcClure

Published by American Robotnik
P.O. Box 42111, Portland, OR 97242, U.S.A.
AmericanRobotnik.com ★ GuerrillaYardwork.com

First edition.
ISBN-13 978-0615764009 ★ ISBN-10: 0615764002

A Note on Gender
English language usage commands adherence to a single gender pronoun throughout a text. In *Guerrilla Yardwork* masculine and feminine gender pronouns alternate to indicate that guerrilla yardwork is for every first-time home and yard owner, regardless of their gender.

A Note on Type
The text of *Guerrilla Yardwork* is set in Baskerville, title and chapter headings in F25 Exclusive, and box quotes in Typewriter Condensed. A classic typeface, Baskerville is renowned for its utility, readability, and agreeability. Both F25 Exclusive and Typewriter Condensed were designed by Volker Busse at F25 Digital Typeface Design in Berlin, Germany. At Dafont.com, where both typefaces were available for free as of December 2012, F25 Exclusive is described as "a remake of a proportional typewriter font" from special 1950's and 1960's typewriters such as IBM Executive.

A Note on Trees
In collaboration with Eco-Libris, one tree will be planted for every paper copy of this book sold. Learn more at ecolibris.net.

Table of Contents

"Nothing is harder
 than armed struggle."
-Sun Tzu

1

Purpose and Politics

Guerrilla yardwork is an irregular, asymmetrical form of yardwork that a home and yard owner performs on his property in conflict against Bad Nature, a large, unwieldy opponent of superior strength (see 1.3.4. Connect to Nature, 2. Theater of Operations, and 3. Combatants). Based on small, repetitive attacks launched at unpredictable times and locations around the yard, guerrilla yardwork utilizes the element of surprise to put a long-lasting, intensive strain on Bad Nature's resources in order to wear down Her resolve, hinder Her operations, and promote Good Nature in Her stead. Offensive, highly mobile, and fluid in character, guerrilla yardwork is marked by swift action of short duration, followed by rapid withdrawal. It employs multiple attacks over a wide area to deceive the enemy and force Her to disperse Her forces.

Guerrilla yardwork applies methods that circumvent or nullify Bad Nature's

"Guerrilla warfare is used by the side which is supported by a majority but which possesses a much smaller number of arms for use in defense against oppression."
-Che Guevara

"Therefore when the battle is joined, The underdog will win."
-Lao Tsu

strengths while exploiting Her weaknesses and co-opting elements of Her forces to meet the insurgent's objectives. A means to an end, guerrilla yardwork aims not to resist Nature as a whole, but to seize power over the yard from Bad Nature and establish control there. Guerrilla yardwork transforms the appearance and function of the yard according to its owner's vision, and, in turn, reflects his personal views, beliefs, values, and attitudes.

1.1. The Guerrilla Yardworker's Purpose

Life philosophy, values, beliefs, personality traits, current circumstances, material and temporal resources, as well as vision and goals for the yard influence the first-time home and yard owner's decision to take up garden tools. Every yardwork guerrilla fights with a different set of motivations and purposes.

"The one strong feature of guerrilla [yardwork] is its quality of internal purity."
-Mao Tse-Tung, re-interpreted

1.1.1. Challenge the Status Quo
The yardwork guerrilla challenges the status quo prevailing in the yard. The radical break from the current state of affairs that she seeks renders her a revolutionary. Guerrilla yardwork constitutes a revolution that every home and yard owner can start. Such a 'yardvolution' may, in fact, be latent in every yard—it just needs a yardvolutionary to ignite it.

1.1.2. Gain Control
If the desire for change is the force pushing the yardwork guerrilla, the wish to control his property is what pulls him. The overarching goal of guerrilla yardwork is to gain, establish, and maintain supremacy over the yard—complete personal

control over the property whereby Bad Nature is incapable of effective interference with the owner's actions.

To establish control over the yard is to exercise power over it. Exercising power and imposing order in his yard manifests the guerrilla yardworker's sense of personal autonomy. Taking action to wrest his yard from Bad Nature's grasp and mold it to his vision expands his freedom to make choices and influence its appearance. The greater the control, the greater the sense of autonomy. The yard is a small parcel of the world that is his and that he can control. To control the yard is to control the world. To be a master of the yard is to be happy.

The psychological impact of shaping a part of the planet cannot be overstated. In many cases, control over the yard offers the guerrilla yardworker a rare opportunity in his life to be in full charge of his actions.

> "Just do what needs to be done.
> Never take advantage of power."
> -Lao Tsu

Paying a gardener or a landscaping company to do the work generates a mediated reality, in which the home and yard owner controls his yard only to the extent his money does. By contrast, the guerrilla yardworker himself creates and retains control over his reality. To see a plant grow from a sapling that he planted into a prosperous bush; to pick tomatoes from a plant he nourished from a start on his window sill; to see daffodils signal each and every spring from the bulbs he stored in the shed all through the winter; in brief, to co-opt Nature with his own hands and a few tools into fulfilling his wishes provides the guerrilla yardworker with satisfaction that only comes from creation.

1.1.3. Escape

The home and yard owner can seek in guerrilla yardwork an escape from her earthly concerns. Her job keeps her in the office, studio, or shop floor for an inordinate amount of time.

Work stress accompanies her home. The mortgage payment weighs both on her budget and mind. A child demands her undivided attention. Her relationship with her spouse or partner generates an additional pressure on her time and energy, as do her relatives, in-laws, and friends. Social obligations such as birthday parties, poetry readings, or concerts test her patience with humanity. The need for repairs, beautification, and upkeep of her home taxes her free time. In a young professional's life, therefore, the yard can become a peaceful place to hide. A productive and inexpensive activity to enjoy at any time, guerrilla yardwork grants the home and yard owner welcome solitude, in which she can listen to music, practice mindfulness, or zone out (see 1.1.8. Experience Flow).

1.1.4. Heed Others' Expectations

The yardwork guerrilla cannot avoid facing his spouse's, partner's, or relatives' expectations for yard improvements (mere maintenance, such as mowing or pruning, tends to fall short). He can thus take up tools simply to please others.

Lacking interest or skills in interior design, cooking, or other indoor activities besides watching sports broadcasts, reading newspapers, and napping, which are generally considered unproductive despite their advantages, the soon-to-be yardwork insurgent likely endures a stream of requests from his *loved one* to contribute to the household with labor. Common statements include, "Get off the couch and build the garden bed," or, "Stop watching TV and get rid of those blackberry bushes." Expectations can come in less direct, more passive-aggressive forms, too. This is the first paradox of guerrilla yardwork: the G.Y. can wage a war in the yard to keep the peace at home.

Parents tend to be proud of their offspring's purchase of his first home. It shows them he is finally a responsible individual capable of taking care of himself and his family—their work as parents is done. However, rather than dissipate, parents' expectations tend to grow following the purchase, particularly if the parents contributed toward the down payment. The bigger their contribution, the greater the expectation. Because they tend to see their financial support as an investment, they anticipate a return in the form of home improvements or other measures that increase the property's value. Indications of disappointment include raised eyebrows, head shaking, occasionally accompanied by a 'tsk-tsk' sound, or expressions such as, "Did you buy the house so we can work on it in our old age?"; "Is this how we raised you?"; and, in extreme circumstances, "We want our money back." Similarly, *in-laws* expect their son's or daughter's spouse to behave like an adult. They, too, wish to see their investment pay off.

In the case of *neighbors* and others, the expectation may be less vocal but it's no less present. Few judgments sound as harsh and damage the yardvolutionary's ego as severely as, "The yard looks exactly the same as it did three years ago." The sentiment need not be spoken; a look of disapproval or a dismissive wave of hand suffices. The home and yard owner who moves in and does nothing raises questions about his character and intentions for the property. It goes against the G.Y.'s ethos to be considered as less than an industrious and diligent member of society (see 1.3.8. Promote Work Ethic) or to raise suspicions about the real motives behind the purchase. Yardvolutionary activity prevents misjudgments and suspicions from arising.

1.1.5. Crack God's Whip

Regardless of her faith, the spiritually-inclined G.Y. can adapt guerrilla yardwork to her beliefs.

For the *Christian* insurgent, the drive to control the yard aligns with the biblical notion of human dominion over the Earth. The G.Y. strives to preserve God's creation; she believes God created the Earth perfect and that it is her duty to protect it. Because guerrilla yardwork is more environmentally friendly than its mainstream alternatives (see 4.4. The Relation of Guerrilla to Regular Yardwork), in addition to 'creation care,' the Christian yardvolutionary curries favor in God's eyes for her method, too. The Christian guerrilla yardworker who sees herself as an instrument in the hands of a higher power (the so-called 'crusader G.Y.') fights to perfect God's creation.

The *Jewish* guerrilla yardworker works in the spirit of *tikkun olam*, or repairing the world, which instructs her to work every day to improve the world, including the natural environment, for 'G-d,' the Earth's eternal and true owner. Similarly, the *Muslim* guerrilla yardworker believes she is Allah's representative on Earth and must care for the environment, which, as a reflection of truth is sacred.

In a general sense, the *Hindu* guerrilla yardworker's conduct is a set of dharmic behaviors, which she performs in order to maintain the natural order of things. Finally, the *Buddhist* guerrilla yardworker strives to remove all her inwardly-focused attachments, the source of her suffering. A humble human, she practices outwardly-focused compassion with all living things, seeks a deeper connection with nature, and pursues balance and harmony with the natural world, including in her yard.

1.1.6. Express Yourself

The new yard never looks exactly the way the new owner wants it to. Unless he takes action, the yard will remain as he first found it, reflecting the previous owner's ideas of beauty and utility. He will wish to transform the newly-acquired space into a home, expressing his personality. Guerrilla yardwork can serve him well in this regard. He contrasts the version of material reality as he discovers it in the yard with his ideal version of it and takes up yard tools to eliminate the difference between them.

1.1.7. Improve Health

Guerrilla yardwork makes its agents physically and mentally stronger individuals. The work the G.Y. performs with her body benefits both her physique and personality. The physical demands of guerrilla yardwork help the guerrilla yardworker develop endurance and build muscle mass. Combined with additional conditioning, e.g. from running, biking, team sports, and stretching, it comprises a balanced, natural exercise regime that requires no gym membership or expensive gear. Higher demand on bodily output leads to higher demand for a more nutritious diet to sustain the effort. Exercising more and eating better, the G.Y. finds herself in superior physical shape and having much more sustained energy.

> "Consult the genius of the place in all;
> That tells the waters or to rise, or fall;
> Or helps th' ambitious hill the heav'ns to scale,
> Or scoops in circling theatres the vale;
> Calls in the country, catches opening glades,
> Joins willing woods, and varies shades from shades,
> Now breaks, or now directs, th' intending lines;
> Paints as you plant, and, as you work, designs."
> –Alexander Pope

Being stronger, leaner, and better nourished positively influences the G.Y.'s overall well-being. Gaining greater control over the yard, seeing her labors come to fruition, and altering the shape of the Earth with her own hands boosts her confidence, strengthens her resolve, and improves her outlook on life. The grizzled look obtained from exposure to the elements adds a valuable side benefit.

1.1.8. Experience Flow

With each winning battle, the yardwork guerrilla becomes more and more immersed in his actions, finding himself 'in the zone' with increasing frequency. Over time, he may find he no longer seeks guerrilla yardwork solely to pursue his original extrinsic motivations, but for its own sake. As expounded by Mihályi Csikszentmihályi, flow is the state of 'optimal experience' which the dedicated guerrilla yardworker experiences when he finds himself so involved in his fight that nothing outside it matters. And, he enjoys the activity for the sheer sake of doing it.

A number of factors accompany the experience of flow:

- Clear and attainable goals align with the G.Y.'s skill.
- He receives direct and immediate feedback about the results of his actions.
- He is in the state of focused concentration and full immersion in the present moment.
- He feels the sense of control over the course and outcomes of his actions.
- He loses self-consciousness, awareness of his own physicality, and the sense of time.
- The action is intrinsically rewarding.

Detractors argue that without a transformational goal the yardvolution disintegrates (see 1.3. The Politics of Guerrilla Yardwork). But the pursuit of flow meshes well with other purposes. It strengthens the yardvolutionary as an individual. Flow experiences yield outcomes superior to those of externally-driven actions. Guerrilla yardworkers who have experienced flow report better results after mindfully concentrating on breathing, muscle movement, and the terrain than when focusing on the achievement of such results. Likewise, the guerrilla yardworker eventually finds he can accomplish more in a day's work and feel more satisfied if he works without any external, predetermined gauge of progress or success.

Related to flow is mindfulness, whereby the guerrilla yardworker brings his attention to the present experience and acknowledges and accepts his current movement, thoughts, feelings, and surroundings with an open mind. Mindfulness requires the return to full attention, awareness, and effort.

Flow and mindfulness are far from being mutually exclusive, however. If the G.Y. goes into battle in a state of mindfulness, she is likely to transition into flow. Seemingly mindless, repetitive tasks like digging or weeding lend themselves well to both mindfulness and flow.

The yardvolutionary war is a long one. The insurgent who fights mindfully and in flow achieves more in less time and derives greater satisfaction from his actions.

1.1.9. Establish a Legacy

When the guerrilla yardworker transforms her yard, she leaves a legacy. First, she plants her vision of the yard in the minds of her spouse, partner, children, family, friends, and neighbors, where it sprouts and grows into its own. Even after she has departed from it, the yard as she made it will live on as a neighborhood legend.

The G.Y.'s legacy extends beyond the yard's physical appearance. Guerrilla yardwork is a way of life, a philosophy that its practitioner puts into practice with every action she takes. She leaves an indelible impression in the minds of all those who watched and supported her. Perhaps she even inspires some to take up tools and follow the guerrilla yardwork path themselves (see. 3.3.3. Recruitment).

The yardvolutionary makes the world a better, more beautiful, and more useful place, both in material reality and in the minds of others—that is her legacy.

1.2. Evolution of Yardvolutionary Purpose

The yardvolutionary struggle transforms the insurgent. As he adopts guerrilla yardwork into his life, the original motivation becomes exhausted. If he undertook the yardvolution to build endurance and strength or to answer a loved one's call, finding greater and greater pleasure in his conduct pushes him to adopt a more meaningful purpose. A conflict arises between his views and his behavior. In order to dispose of the cognitive dissonance, the guerrilla yardworker explores the philosophy that underlies the method and subsequently adopts a new, higher purpose. The immediate and long-term rewards of guerrilla yardwork inspire the G.Y. to adopt its philosophical and practical tenets; thereafter, he continues the fight from the heart. Closely intertwined, internal and external motivations for starting the yardvolution evolve as they give rise to one another or blend into various combinations.

"Nothing can bring you peace but the triumph of principles."
-Ralph Waldo Emerson

"Without a political goal, guerrilla warfare must fail. The essence of guerrilla warfare is revolutionary in character."
-Mao Tse-Tung

1.3. The Politics of Guerrilla Yardwork

Guerrilla yardwork has a distinct political dimension. In her yard, the guerrilla yardworker is a powerful but lone force for change. It is on the aggregate level, across all the yards being transformed, that the yardvolution achieves its full potential.

As a dictionary term, 'revolution' means both a radical change and a return to the original state of affairs. Guerrilla yardwork's practitioners aim to achieve both.

1.3.1. Exact Change

Through guerrilla yardwork, the first-time home and yard owner molds the yard's physical appearance, alters its character, and improves its utility according to his unique personal vision. The difference between the initial and envisioned states of the yard determines the radicality of change. A well-maintained yard that balances productive and recreational areas focuses the fortunate guerrilla yardworker's struggle on tweaking its aesthetics and on maintenance. An outdated, neglected, or unusable yard calls for a full-scale conflict.

Guerrilla yardwork declares that change is both necessary and possible: the yard, the neighborhood, and the city can benefit. Members of guerrilla yardworker bands affect urban change on a grand scale. With their bodies and minds, they move the earth according to their wishes.

The cause-and-effect relationship between the guerrilla's actions and the change in the yard creates a new reality not just in the yard but also in himself. When "I should" turns into "I can" and "I paid someone to do this" to "I did this with my own hands," every insurgent internalizes the idea that he has the power to improve the world. He no longer has to wait for the do-gooders, the government, or his charitable contributions to 'make a difference.' He himself can.

"[T]he guerrilla has the intention of destroying an unjust order and therefore an intention to replace the old with something new."
–Che Guevara

The improved body and the mind of every guerrilla change the cultural composition of entire communities. Increased individual empowerment and self-efficacy that result from guerrilla yardwork help combat personal entitlement, narcissistic culture, and consumerism that have gripped the nation in recent decades. Change is thus possible in the social realm, as well: spouses and partners, relatives and friends, neighbors and passersby, coworkers and teammates can all experience the effects of guerrilla yardwork. By modeling a new sort of behavior, yardvolutionaries affect bottom-up social change of unparalleled proportions.

1.3.2. Re-Establish Equality

Guerrilla yardwork is an equalizer. Real estate ownership realizes a part of the American Dream, but it carries a hefty price: house poverty. Being young and having limited savings (see 3.1.1. Objective Characteristics of the Yardwork Guerrilla), first-time home and yard owners tend to purchase properties in need of improvement. When a large proportion of total household income goes toward mortgage payments, property taxes, insurance, utilities, upkeep, and improvement, little funds remain for discretionary budget items.

The novice home and yard owner must keep her head up and find inexpensive or free ways to turn her property into a home. Guerrilla yardwork offers one such path: it provides a set of strategies and tactics that require only a small initial investment for basic equipment and supplies (see 5.1.5. Arm Yourself: Yardwork Guerrilla's Equipment), and only incremental outlays over a longer period. Most of the expense for guerrilla yardwork comes in the form of time and labor.

As a practice, guerrilla yardwork levels the field of urban-residence proprietors. It enables everyone to bypass the limitations that home and yard ownership imposes and to create a beautiful and productive yard on any budget.

1.3.3. Reclaim the Self

Guerrilla yardwork returns humans to themselves and to the world. Reliance on fossil fuels and uranium has separated us from natural sources of energy (sun, wind, and muscle), and helped technology accelerate human events to an unprecedented degree. Rather than adapting machines to the limits of our humanity, we live at the speed of the machines we created. We are all the worse for it.

The acceleration of our lives has come hand in hand with the takeover of time, as Venkatesh Rao and many others have shown. Every human being owns the subjective, mental dimension of experience that constitutes time. At the first glance, faster machines suggest greater availability of time, but even though time-saving devices, like the washing machine or the automobile, free up time in one area of our lives, we are immediately redirected to consuming other technology, particularly the entertainment media and luxury goods.

Guerrilla yardwork allows the first-time home and yard owner to slow down and reclaim time. By decelerating to the speed of his muscles, the shovel and the hoe, the sun and the rain, he returns to the mental space he lost in the digital whirlwind. He replaces sacrificing at the altar of speed with living a life of quiet contemplation. He ditches noise and distraction for silence and concentration. He changes from a mindless, machine-controlled drone to a thoughtful, self-determined human being. By ridding himself of the ties that preoccupy him as he flitters from screen to screen, window to window, tab to tab, he reclaims the ties that bind him to humanity. In the yard, it's just him, his tools, and his land. He has all the time in the world to act or to waylay, to work or to sit idle, to stick his hands in the dirt or to stare at the clouds. He returns to the privacy of his thoughts. He repossesses his time.

In addition, humans have become enmeshed with the systems the machines constitute, which have become embedded in our lives so much that it is difficult to fathom living without or outside them. As Marshal McLuhan presaged decades ago, technology is no longer something we do—it's something we are part of, something that owns us. We have amputated not just our senses but ourselves as well. We replaced our souls with artificial total prostheses; we replaced ourselves with automatons; we replaced our environment with a network of machines that envelops and encompasses us. We made ourselves passive and dependent. We live our lives vicariously through our digital tools and through our own reflections in them. Immersed in augmented realities, virtual relationships, and gigabytes of data, we live ever more efficiently, away from real, inefficient events, objects, and people. We are removed from the world as it exists outside our windows.

The yardwork guerrilla refuses to increase his entanglement with technology and with other people via technology. He rejects constant digital connectedness that asks him to participate in a universe of self-promotion, to always broadcast himself, to surrender his soul in exchange for a dopamine squirt, to never unplug. He denounces the data-driven life of a cyborg. Instead, he re-establishes a clear line between what is human/natural and what is human-made/artificial.

The extensive use of digital technology has created a culture of distraction and multitasking, both of which boost stress, intensify confusion and fatigue, and accelerate aging. The human brain remembers and learns less. Our ability to focus and analyze is compromised. As tasks multiply and as switching between them accelerates, each task becomes harder to complete and the process of its completion more easily forgotten. We do without being, go without experiencing, act without remembering.

By contrast, the yardwork guerrilla fights only one battle at a time, and even then only one that he can win (see 4.2.4. Preserve Yourself). The singular focus on the task at hand requires deep concentration that easily transitions into flow or mindfulness (see 1.1.8. Experience Flow). It eases the mind and makes each moment memorable. The guerrilla yardworker does not just do, he is—he experiences, he remembers.

With rapid technological progress and commercial application of science humans have also become accustomed to using machines without understanding how they operate. The connection between cause and effect is lost in the automatic, digital magic. We are passive, dependent consumers, rather than active, independent producers.

Guerrilla yardwork reconnects humans to age-old tools they can fully comprehend: everyone understands the shovel, the wheelbarrow, or the rake. The yardvolutionary can feel their shape and their weight in his hands. As he uses these tools, every muscle and every sense register his actions and their immediate consequences. He is no longer a tool of his tools—he is their master. He also recognizes himself in the results of his work. With simple extensions of his body, the yardwork guerrilla becomes one with himself and the planet, able to alter both for the better.

> "Man follows the earth.
> Earth follows heaven."
> –Lao Tsu

Guerrilla yardwork is a politics of the body and the mind. By becoming one with the environment, the G.Y. reclaims the power to directly influence the world's workings. He ceases to be an instrument in the screen's eyes and transforms himself into an agent of change using simple tools. In the course of his struggle, he regains the freedom to do what he wants, when he wants. (To be sure, time, space, and money do constrain his freedom: his yard is only so big and he has only so much disposable income. But the yard can be used as a base for the expansion of freedom into other realms of his life.)

Since it amounts to slow landscaping and gardening, guerrilla yardwork combats the culture of instant gratification. By eschewing heavy machinery, industrial fertilizers, genetically modified plants, and artificial materials it espouses traditional ways of tending to land. Its focus on native plants promotes the thriving of the local ecosystem (in many cases, a dedicated guerrilla yardworker can turn his backyard into a certified wildlife habitat).

Finally, because guerrilla yardwork tends to be an urban phenomenon (see 3.4. Relationship to the City), the city exerts a multitude of pressures on the first-time home and yard owner. Georg Simmel has shown that the acceleration of life, the multiplication and intensification of sensory stimuli, the frequent changes in the environment, and other vagaries of urban existence profoundly disrupt the urban dweller's psyche.

"Love the world as your own self; then you can truly care for all things."
—Lao Tsu

By empowering the first-time home and yard owner to control his actions, guerrilla yardwork allows him to resist being chewed, swallowed, and regurgitated by the city's social and technological mechanisms, to live a deeper existence, and to retain (or regain) his independence as a human being. It brings him closer to himself, closer to other people, and closer to the Earth. This is the second paradox of guerrilla yardwork: it can thrive in the built environment while providing a refuge from it.

The power shift from technology and to humanity becomes especially evident on the aggregate scale. The same way a meadow grows from a myriad of flowers, the cumulative effect of individual yardvolutions is considerable: when the yardvolutionary army takes back the power they gradually surrendered in exchange for civilization's comforts, they become true to themselves, true to their loved ones and their fellow citizens, true to Good Nature and to the Earth.

1.3.4. Connect to Nature
Guerrilla yardwork brings the G.Y. into the light. He no longer casts his eyes downward at the computer monitor, television screen, or GPS navigation system, but up, at the tree crowns, the sky, the birds. Rather than having light shine from the machine into his eyes, he sees the world in natural light, watches it change as the Sun travels across the sky, shifting the angle,

the hue, the shadows throughout the day and with the seasons. He no longer relies on the buzz of the alarm clock but awakens when the birds begin to chirp or chickens to cluck. Even when he's moving rocks or kneeling in the dirt, his sight is in constant motion, taking in his surroundings. The fresh air, the Earth's scents, the passage of the clouds, the rustle of grass fill him with joy. The world becomes crisper; he wiser and more fulfilled. Sometimes, he can hear the tomatoes ripen.

On the grand scale, the yardvolutionary troops' shift of attention from their screens into their yards reignites their consciousness and reunites them with the planet. As they see their flowers blossom, they make a thousand triumphant returns.

The third paradox of guerrilla yardwork: at the same time that he seeks to re-merge with Nature, the guerrilla yardworker considers Her bad parts—Bad Nature—the enemy, fighting harmful, foreign, or unnecessary elements. Removing ivy, bamboo, or dandelions clears Nature of invasive plants that stifle the growth of others—all plants that hurt beneficial ones must go. It rids it of plants that belong on another continent—all plants that are not native to his climate must go. It removes stubborn specimens that have no place in his plans—all plants that clash with his vision for the yard must go. Parallel to revolutionary change he seeks to enact in his yard, he fights for a restoration to a state as original as he can create. He seeks to establish the rule of Good Nature. Thus, as the guerrilla strives to return to his roots in Nature, he also works to compel Nature to return to Her good self.

1.3.5. Grow Food, Achieve Self-Sufficiency
Whether it's from a single plant, a garden bed, or a row stretching across her property, the guerrilla yardworker can enjoy every fruit or vegetable in her yard. This brings advantages.

The fruit and vegetable gardener participates in the entire life cycle of produce. She knows where her food comes from, how it was grown, and where the scraps will go. Yard farming wrests power from the food production and distribution industries into her hands. It also boosts her self-reliance and weaves food into her everyday life in a more meaningful way.

In contrast to wage labor, whereby the value of her work's surplus flows to someone else (owner, shareholders, organization), the yardwork guerrilla keeps the surplus she produced. Not having to buy produce saves her money and time she'd spend shopping. She also eats more fruits and vegetables.

Providing for herself through her labor rather than with the monetary means of exchange can be very empowering to the G.Y. The autonomy she gains from growing her food fuels her motivation for guerrilla yardwork.

"Growing food is a hugely uplifting experience. It can be a spiritual as well as edible antidote to an otherwise debilitating environment."
-Richard Reynolds

In many cases, e.g. during the tomato season or apple harvest, the yard can produce more than the household needs at the moment or than can be pickled or preserved. The yardwork guerrilla can donate her surplus to friends and family as offerings during visits, use it as contributions to potlucks, or exchange it in barter transactions for produce she lacks (apricots for gherkins and basil for edible flowers have been shown to be particularly satisfactory trades).

Food grown in the yard is healthier and tastier. Taking minimal time from harvest to mouth, it is the freshest food possible. The G.Y. uses no chemicals to cultivate it. No nutrients get lost in storage or transit.

Growing her own food allows for preparing meals based on fruits or vegetables that are in season. Eating what nature provides on a given day, supplementing it with store-bought ingredients, teaches the guerrilla yardworker to do the best she can with what she has on hand. She learns to adapt to Good Nature's rhythms, accept Her generosity, and truly accli-

Fig. 1   "Man follows the earth. Earth follows heaven."

mate to the local conditions. She adopts the strategic posture of self-reliance, which further encourages her personal empowerment. Relying on her own hard work to feed herself makes her a stronger individual; if she barters the surplus from her yard with the surplus from the yards of her fellow guerrillas, it strengthens the entire community.

On larger scale, home-grown food improves communities by increasing the overall food supply in the zone. Particularly in urban areas known as food deserts, where wholesome affordable food is difficult to obtain or altogether unavailable, growing produce in the yard contributes to overall food security and safety. It also bolsters urban biodiversity and beauty of the neighborhood, lowers the home and yard owner's carbon footprint, and requires minimal driving and no packaging.

1.3.6. Exercise Frugality

Hand in hand with self-reliance comes frugality. Having labored in the yard, the guerrilla yardworker values the food he brings to the table more than the food he buys. He comes to appreciate and use more resourcefully everything he has. He learns to use the produce from his yard and all the other consumables efficiently and economically, with minimum waste. He practices fiscal self-restraint, buying only what he truly needs. He refrains from purchasing extravagant products or feeding costly habits. Being able to do yardwork himself contributes to his bottom line, including savings.

1.3.7. Improve Community Health

The guerrilla yardworker improves her and her community's health through both the fruits of her labor and the process of growing them. Changes in bodily input (food) and output (exercise) resulting from guerrilla yardwork get the insurgent in great physical and mental shape (see 5.5.1. Cultivation of Health). By improving her health and by modeling healthy behavior, she turns into an unwitting agent of community health improvement.

Aside from boosting health in general, guerrilla yardwork also helps fight the obesity epidemic. The guerrilla yardworker soon finds that not only does she lack time to indulge in watching television, gaming, or other sedentary activities, her body rejects unhealthy food. Fatty, sugary, processed, and artificial substances trigger feelings of sluggishness, exhaustion, and laziness. Guerrilla yardwork weeds out fat and prevents the return to an unhealthy lifestyle; it becomes a healthy addiction.

The psychological effects of guerrilla yardwork cannot be underestimated. Feeling good physically, spending time outdoors, and gaining a sense of autonomy contribute to improved mental strength and life satisfaction. The I-can-do-anything spirit springing from guerrilla yardwork reinforces what's best about America. By strengthening themselves, members of the guerrilla yardworker army bolster the strength of their communities and of the nation as a whole.

1.3.8. Change the Urban Aesthetic

Guerrilla yardwork transforms the city. As the insurgent enacts change in his yard, he also affects the appearance of the environment beyond its boundaries. Each modification of the yard, no matter how small or temporary, contributes to the change in the block's, street's, neighborhood's, and city's aesthetic and function. These gradual changes reach far and deep: changes in each yard ripple through the city's character. The yardvolution is an urban revolution (see 2.3.1. Urban Yards).

The guerrilla yardworker eschews the manicured lawn, the hanging pelargonium, the topiary. The straight line leads to doom. Instead, he strives to approximate in his yard the appearance

"[The yardwork guerrilla] takes care of all things
And abandons nothing."
-Lao Tsu, re-interpreted

of his climate zone's wilderness, while seeking to balance it with productive uses. Planting without a plan, sowing during a spare moment, or trimming on a whim can, over time, create an impression of the yard being a slice of Nature rather than its landscaped simulacrum.

The army of guerrilla yardworkers creates pockets of Good Nature in urban environments. Yard by yard, they quietly transform both the world's appearance and its idea of beauty and utility, setting an example for remaking the American city.

1.3.9. Promote Work Ethic

By promoting the ethic of hard work, guerrilla yardwork rekindles the spirit of American industriousness. It is the insurgent himself, rather than mercenaries—landscaping crews, gardeners, or neighborhood kids—who turns his vision into reality; the yardvolution cannot be outsourced. Because guerrilla yardwork entails manual labor over a considerable period of time, as a way of life it combats sloth, idleness, and purposeless, passive existence. In fact, the yardvolution is so enjoyable an activity that the guerrilla yardworker considers it anything but work. The only potato the guerrilla yardworker becomes is the one he harvests from his yard.

The guerrilla soon finds that once he puts all the yard systems in place, his workload diminishes. No more mowing the lawn every other week; no more daily watering; no more edging. Major transformational projects give way to maintenance and updating. He has only to keep Nature in the yard within the limits he imposed under his vision. Hard work in the short run can, therefore, lead to less work in the long run (see 5.2.2. Tactical Maneuvers).

The ethic of hard work enhances the guerrilla yardworker's character and strengthens the nation. The yardvolutionary recognizes that success in his struggle requires a sturdy personality, and he knows that it can only be achieved through diligence. Through his struggle he manifests the moral benefits of hard work (he is working for himself and the planet), acquires new skills, and develops additional virtues like persistence, perseverance, and productivity. The whole society benefits.

1.3.10. Redeem Humanity

As an admirer of Nature and a keen observer of history, the yardwork insurgent acknowledges environmental degradation humans have wrought upon the planet. She applies the principles of guerrilla yardwork to absolve herself and the entire human kind for the errors of their ways. She sacrifices her body, time, and treasure to steer the course of humanity back on the right track and protect it from damning itself to extinction. A pragmatic idealist at heart, she seeks to leave the world a better place than she found it.

Because of her limited resources, the G.Y. can contribute only her own actions to remedying the state of the natural world. Any machinery she uses must have as little negative environmental impact as possible. She uses no chemicals or other artificial, unnatural, or otherwise harmful substances.

When the guerrilla yardworker takes up her tools, she seeks to enact change for everyone's benefit. Each yard that is more beautiful and fruitful than before makes the world a better place. The proof comes in words of appreciation or thanks from neighbors or passersby for improving her front-yard; from family or friends for the flowers or fruit; from her own conscience for doing good. It appears with the birds flying to feed or frolic in the yard; in the bloom of flowers, bushes, and trees; in the rustle of tree leaves.

The G.Y. can fix her sliver of the world with her own hands. Of course, by itself her war is but a drop in the garden pail of atonement. On the aggregate, however, the actions of the entire

> "Guerrilla [yardwork is] the basis of the struggle of a people to redeem itself."
> -Che Guevara, re-interpreted

guerrilla yardworker army provide a foundation for humanity to redeem itself. Yard by yard, guerrilla yardwork makes the world whole again.

2

Theater of Operations

Superb knowledge of the yard's ground belongs to the essential requirements of guerrilla yardwork. Knowledge is power; intimacy with the battlefield prior to engaging the enemy affects the outcome of battle. The yardwork insurgent must know the terrain to plot his approach, determine the best form and time of attack, and establish the lines of escape. He must familiarize himself with the flora, fauna, and people in the zone.

"Those who don't know the lay of the land cannot maneuver their forces."

"Act after having made assessments. The one who first knows the measures of far and near wins."
–Sun Tzu

2.1. The Yard Defined

The yard, guerrilla yardwork's primary theater of operations, is a plot of land enclosed by a fence or other boundary, directly adjacent to a residential structure, i.e. a house. Though the word itself has the same root as 'garden,' the American garden is typically a subset of the yard in that it is an area that contains one or more plots where vegetables, herbs, flowers, or ornamental plants are grown; other yard subsets may include a lawn, a play area, and a patio.

How many yards are available for guerrilla yardwork in the United States? In 2011 first-time home buyers totaled about 1.9 million people (see 3.3.1. The Size of the Yardvolutionary Army). About two thirds of first-time home and yard buyers purchased real estate properties as couples; it's safe to assume that first-timers purchased roughly 1.2 million properties. Seventy-seven percent of all such properties were single-family detached homes, which brings the total of yards to about 925,000. The median size of properties purchased by first-timers shrank after the Great Recession of 2008-2009: in 2011 first-timers bought homes averaging 1,570 square feet. Because homes seem to take precedence over yards in available data, median lot size can be only estimated. Using an educated guess of average yard size of 8,000 square feet, in 2011, therefore, some 7.4 billion square feet (205,500 acres or 265 square miles) of land was potentially available for yardvolutions. Every year a new batch of yards grows the pool, so if average duration of each yard revolution (6 years, see 3.1.1. Objective Characteristics of the Yardwork Guerrilla) is multiplied by even the low yard area total of 2011, more than 44 billion square feet (1.2 million acres or almost 1,600 square miles) of yard area can be revolutionized at any moment. This represents approximately 1.5% of developed land in the United States of America. The yardvolution is not only widely distributed, it covers a lot of Earth.

To assure victory, the G.Y. must take into consideration numerous spatial and environmental characteristics of his yard. Yards differ by location, type, shape, size, and terrain.

2.2. Climate Zone

The yard's climate zone affects the character and length of the growing season (the average number of days between the last frost in spring and the first frost in fall). Climate zones differ by

- Latitude
- Elevation
- Seasonal highs, lows, and averages
- Precipitation and the resulting humidity or aridity
- Proximity to ocean or to mountains and hills
- Continental air influence
- Microclimates

Though not technically a climate condition, soil also factors heavily in plant development.

Several climate-zone classifications compete for the guerrilla's analytical attention. The United States Department of Agriculture bases its system of hardiness zones on winter low temperatures: the lower the zone number, from 1 to 11, the colder the winter (zones 2 to 10 are split into two), and each zone is warmer by $10°F$ ($-12°C$) than the previous one. The USDA zone system works better for the eastern half of the U.S., which is flatter and which features less complex weather patterns than the West. Taking the opposite approach, the American Horticultural Society builds its 12-zone system on the average number of heat days—temperatures above $86°F$ ($30°C$), at which plants begin suffering physiological damage from heat. The Sunset Western Garden Book uses the broad range of factors listed above to divide the U.S. western seaboard (states west of the Rocky Mountains) into 24 climate zones, with several of the zones divided further into sub-zones, and three additional zones specific to Alaska and two to Hawaii. Depending on his yard's location, the smart guerrilla yardworker combines the climate zone systems to improve the accuracy of his situational assessment.

The guerrilla yardworker must also consider the season of the year, plants native or most suitable for his zone, and his climate zone's fauna. Shoulder seasons—short periods between growing and non-growing seasons when light frost may occur without affecting cool-season crops—are transitional periods during which any kind of yardwork is possible, albeit with some limitations. Spring, summer, autumn, and winter suit different sets of tasks; knowing each season's characteristics helps the yardwork guerrilla shape his operations (the year's seasons closely relate to the growing season). Similarly, knowing what plants are native to his climate zone makes the fight a lot easier. Knowing the animals that pass through, use, or reside in his yard also affects the yardvolution's course: some creatures will warrant feeding, some will best be ignored, and a minority will require expulsion or termination.

Books, such as the aforementioned *Sunset Western Garden Book*; magazines and websites dedicated to gardening; and people in the zone, particularly fellow guerrilla yardworkers, can supply information about the climate zone's characteristics. In addition, continuous observation allows gaining intimate knowledge of the yard's microclimate (see 5.1.2. Explore Battle Terrain).

2.3. Relationship to the City

Yards also differ by their location relative to the built environment of cities and towns. Urban, suburban, and rural yards each present their specific advantages and challenges.

2.3.1. Urban Yards

While guerrilla yardwork can be conducted in any yard, it remains primarily an urban phenomenon. The urban character of guerrilla yardwork derives from the concentration in cities of first-time home and yard owners, the presence of yards most suitable to yardvolutionary struggle, and the support system for continuous, long-term combat.

The yardwork guerrilla must first assess the city's physical characteristics. Heat emanating from buildings and pavement, water directed into sewers and rivers, and air pollution help create microclimates altering the natural characteristics of the yard's climate zone. Higher population and building density means shorter travel distances, more inconvenient (and hence less) driving, more walking and more frequent use of alternative transportation—all of which boost both the amount of time available for guerrilla yardwork and the insurgent's health. Residential areas tend to be built around a traffic grid, which provides for less traffic congestion and time spent in traffic. The city boasts more people who can potentially constitute the yardwork guerrilla's support system. In other words, the yardwork guerrilla is surrounded by other yardwork guerrillas. Greater proximity of amenities and stores, more efficient supply and escape routes, greater availability of disposable time, and superior health outcomes combine into a favorable environment.

"The moral superiority is what sustains the urban guerrilla. Thanks to it, the urban guerrilla can accomplish his principal duty, which is to attack and to survive."
–Carlos Marighella

The culture of the city and its neighborhoods presents an additional backdrop to the yardvolution. Social pressures affect the yardwork guerrilla's freedom and range of operations, the breadth and depth of her support base, and, therefore, her ultimate success. By way of gross generalization: in cosmopolitan, liberal ('blue'), or younger cities (or such pockets in any city), which tend to have more progressive or loose aesthetic standards, the G.Y. will encounter weaker public resistance to her ways than in more traditionalist, conservative ('red'), or demographically older communities, where she fights as a true vanguard of revolutionary yard change. She must, therefore, become familiar with the people in the zone, including the demographic, social, and economic composition of her neighborhood, and act accordingly. The yardwork guerrilla's success hinges on the support of her immediate circle, with her spouse or partner, friends, family, or work colleagues providing different levels and kinds of assistance. Neighbors are of utmost importance in the struggle—even a single old-fashioned neighbor in a predominantly young or liberal neighborhood can create uncomfortable situations with questions, complaints, or staring. Paradoxically, neighbors that are generally considered bad provide the fewest objections to guerrilla yardwork due to a low level of concern for their surroundings; on the other hand, such bad neighbors cannot be relied upon to provide support when needed.

Culturally the city offers advantages over other areas:

- The proximity of the yardwork guerrilla's personal support network creates a dependable operational rear and a plethora of sanctuaries in time of need.
- The presence and movement of a large number of people in a relatively small area produces an atmosphere of anonymity and detachment, even among close neighbors, that the yardwork guerrilla can exploit.
- Looser aesthetic standards create more room for the G.Y. to dream big; they also provide for greater flexibility in realizing her yardvolutionary dream.

Finally, legal requirements for home and yard owners, too, constrain operational freedom. The city may require residential property owners to maintain passable the right of way areas, to mow or otherwise care for medians between the sidewalk and the street, or to remove leaves fallen on the street. The limits on her actions will be even more severe if the yardwork guerrilla belongs to a Home Owners Association. An HOA's covenants, conditions, and restrictions may dictate overall yard appearance and design, including allowed and banned plants, number of certain plants, or a properly maintained lawn; restrict yard activities, dust, smell, and noise; or prescribe maintenance schedules, fence or hedge sizes, or items prohibited in the yard. As a general rule, therefore, the guerrilla yardworker avoids purchasing her home and yard in a zone governed by an HOA.

2.3.2. Suburban Yards

The suburb is a separate outlying residential area of a city or a separate municipality, borough, or unincorporated area outside a city, within a commuting distance of a city. Lower suburban population density correlates with larger yards surrounding predominantly single-family dwellings.

Though suburban land tends to be flat to allow for easy construction and access, other suburban characteristics constrain the yardvolutionary struggle. Lower population density and the lack of a center or walkable neighborhoods dictate the suburban supply system be decentralized into shopping malls, strip malls, and 'big box' stores, all of which require more driving for necessities. Longer distances require more driving. Because the suburban traffic system relies on a less efficient hierarchy of collector roads, the suburban insurgent spends more time in traffic congestions. More driving reduces the guerrilla's disposable time (the average one-way commute is close to 25 minutes), weakens her social support networks, and leads to negative health outcomes, such as recurrent pain, increased stress, and obesity.

The suburban culture disconnects people in the zone from their environment. The suburban yardvolutionary soon discovers a dearth of kindred spirits to join or support her in the struggle. Suburban isolation severely hampers the chances for revolutionary yard transformation. Neighbor peer pressure forces a potential G.Y. into visual conformity of manicured lawns and meticulous, uniform yard upkeep. The oft-reported dullness, artificiality, and predictability of suburban landscape hamper any effort to act outside the 'little box.' No revolution has originated in the suburbs, where people settle for a quieter, safer, and more spacious life.

In order to decide whether to take a chance on suburban life, the first-time home and yard owner who is considering starting a yardvolution should investigate the area in greater depth. Conversations with suburbanites can offer insights into the local population's psyche; drives, field visits, or parties can reveal details of the physical environment; and research of secondary resources can expand interpretational and analytical depth (see Sources and Inspirations).

A special case of the suburban battlefield is the exurban, commuter town, located beyond the suburban boundary, which people use as a base for commuting to the city or suburb for wage labor. Such bedroom communities tend to be formerly independent, self-standing towns that became connected with the city as built environment sprawled. Drive times eat into disposable time even more than in the case of suburbs; traditionalist aesthetic values are even more likely; and, in subdivisions, yards tend to be small. Culture in exurban communities can isolate the brave yardwork guerrilla as an oddball, compromising the revolutionary nature of her struggle and leaving her without a functioning support system. The exurb accentuates the suburb's disadvantages; an exurban yardwork guerrilla is an oxymoron.

2.3.3. Rural Yards

Yards in rural areas are the least conducive to guerrilla yard-work. Cultural and demographic constraints tend to exceed those of suburbs. The G.Y. can rarely count on the local population to support her struggle. Rural areas feature large land tracts and are sparsely populated. Even though legal restrictions may be looser than in urban or suburban zones, square footage can prohibit transforming and maintaining the yard without motorized machinery. Long distances require extended driving on narrow roads. Infrastructure is dispersed. The rural environment tends to disfavor guerrilla yardwork.

2.4. Yard Characteristics

Many characteristics define yards. Some are more important, such as lot location or terrain, others matter less, such as the type of home the yard surrounds. All, however, impact the strategy and tactics of guerrilla yardwork in some way.

2.4.1. Lot Location

Residential areas in American cities tend to consist of rectangular blocks. As a result, the urban yard can be located in either a surrounded or a corner lot.

The *surrounded yard* faces the street with only one side—the front. Neighboring lots abut the surrounded lot on each side and in the back. Front and back yards are clearly delineated. A narrow strip of land adjoins at least one side of the dwelling, forming a side yard that provides access between front and back yards.

The surrounded lot comes with two sets of neighbors. The side neighbors have clearer sight lines to both the front yard and, depending on the type of fence, the back yard. The side neighbors' proximity generates more opportunities for learning and sharing through constructive conversation; the guerrilla can attempt to affect change there by serving as a role model of revolutionary yard change. Conversely, because on each side of the surrounded lot the yardwork guerrilla encounters a yard that's different from his, he can gain valuable insights from each of them and their owners. The back neighbor is typically of less concern, as the G.Y.'s rear fence doubles as his rear fence.

The surrounded lot can create an oppressed feel if the neighboring houses sit too close. On the other hand, tight quarters can spur the guerrilla yardworker's creativity in combat.

The *corner lot yard* is directly adjacent to the intersection of two streets. Only two other lots abut it; the facade of the house prescribes that the lot next to it be the side lot and the one behind the house the back lot.

Because the corner lot borders on two streets, many inexperienced guerrillas consider it a tough battlefield. The corner yard is more exposed to the elements on the side that borders the street and hence more vulnerable to unpredictable outside attacks, such as vandalism or littering. The strip of land stretching from the street corner down the side boundary adds to the home and yard owner's responsibilities. The length of the privacy fence suitable or desired for some corner lots may create a closed-in feel in the yard.

The corner lot's principal advantage outweighs the drawbacks. Because the corner lot has only two neighbors, there is a lesser chance of disagreement, dispute, or conflict. Particularly the rear neighbor will be of little concern. As a result, the guerrilla yardworker with a corner lot may, in effect, have only one neighbor to contend with and, therefore, be afforded greater operational freedom.

2.4.2. Yard Boundary
Because the urban yard surrounds a dwelling, it has both an inner and an outer boundary. The yard's inner boundary com-

prises the edges of the house and other structures present in the property, such as a garage, shed, or granny unit (in recent years, green roofs have sprung up, extending the yard *onto* the house or other structures). The yard's outer boundary represents the geographic and legal limit of combat. Containing the yard insurgency within the yard boundary keeps the peace with both the neighbors and authorities. Upon seizing possession of the property, the prudent guerrilla yardworker confirms all property lines with measurements against the city's official map, with property pins buried in the ground, or with the help of a licensed land surveyor. In most cases property lines will already be set by fences, sidewalks, walls, or other markers.

A vertical barrier delineates the yard boundary and serves other important functions:

- Security (keeping things out)
- Containment (keeping things in)
- Privacy (keeping eyes away)
- Noise reduction (keeping sound down)
- Peace-keeping
- Decoration (keeping things beautiful)

Both boundary material and style affect these functions. The selection of barrier type allows the G.Y. to influence the course of the yardvolution, particularly in areas close to the boundary, and shape the outcome of the yard's transformation.

Plant barriers, such as a row of trees (live fencing) or shrubs (hedge), while fairly permeable, provide an aesthetically pleasing, natural backdrop for the yardwork insurgency. Tall and thick hedgerows provide excellent privacy protection, noise reduction, and intrusion prevention. Because natural barriers add to the guerrilla yardworker's duties, he selects plants that require minimum maintenance, such as acacia, holly, or prickly pear.

Fence is the most common boundary marker in urban residential areas. City regulations may prescribe maximum fence heights, with front fences shorter and back fences taller. Most guerrilla yardworkers leave the front yard fenceless to create a sense of openness and to impress that they have nothing to hide. Fencelessness also creates greater freedom of movement. The side and back fences typically function as privacy barriers. The function, height, and type of fence between neighbors may be a matter of mutual agreement, as the best-case scenario, or a simple one-sided exercise of property rights, which is less ideal. Some neighbors tolerate a maximum-height privacy fence, others contend with a shorter fence to retain a sense of open space. The adage, "Good fences make good neighbors," applies with full force: a truly good fence is one that both sides enjoy. The law may require adjacent landowners to share the responsibility for maintaining the common boundary.

Fences come in numerous styles and materials. Wood fences are typical of urban residential areas. To arrest deterioration, particularly in rainy or humid climates and close to the ground, the G.Y. chooses pressure-treated wood for posts and rails, and decay-resistant wood, such as cedar, for vertical boards (pickets). He extends the lifespan of his wood fence with a water repellent or a wood preservative (the yardwork guerrilla only uses natural materials) and by keeping rails and pickets off the ground.

Common wood fence styles include:

- *Split* or *post-and-rail fence.* Horizontal wood pieces are inserted into vertical posts. Plastic is occasionally substituted for wood, especially in rainy or humid climate zones. Because the split fence is highly permeable and provides little security or other protection, it is typically used for decorative purposes in the front yard.

- *Picket fence.* Approximately waist-high, the picket fence is easily breached and, therefore, typically used for decorative purposes in the front yard.
- *Solid* or *stockade fence.* With tightly spaced pickets nailed to horizontal rails that connect four-by-four posts inserted into the ground, the solid fence provides excellent privacy protection and moderate security. Over time, pickets may shrivel, creating gaps that compromise privacy. Security can be slightly improved by affixing a string of barbed wire along the top edge or, if a rail tops the pickets, a row of nails nailed through the rail's bottom side. However, because such measures may attract undue attention, the yardwork insurgent avoids them and supplants their function with greater vigilance and monitoring.
- *Shadowbox.* Pickets alternate front and back to achieve uniform look on both sides. This type of fencing eliminates the decorative disadvantage of the solid fence, whose less appealing side with exposed rails can create a sense of enclosedness within the yard. The shadowbox fence offsets the visual appeal with visual penetrability: while privacy is assured from the right angle, lower angles reveal gaps between the inner and outer vertical boards, opening various portions of the yard to visual inspection. Otherwise, the shadowbox fence has the same advantages and disadvantages as the stockade fence.
- *Lattice.* Used instead of pickets, it offers a superior decorative advantage. It is slightly lower in cost than solid or shadowbox fences but comes with inferior privacy and noise protection.

A low-cost alternative to the wood fence, the chain-link fence, features metal wires woven together in a diamond pattern. It offers weak privacy protection and creates an impression of cheapness. Wrought-iron fences are used for decorative purposes, usually in the front yard. Other fence types and materials, such as barbed wire, electric fence, or vinyl, are less common in residential areas; the yardwork guerrilla may encounter them if his property borders land zoned for commercial use. Even less common are palisades, wattles, bamboo, and other creative fence styles.

Solid materials, e.g. concrete, rock, or brick, resist the elements to the greatest degree. Depending on height, they also provide the highest level of privacy and sound protection. However, walls can create an oppressive feeling of enclosure, clashing with the yardwork insurgency's aim to break through figurative walls. Solid-wall fences are best suited for decoration (rocks, slate), to retain higher ground (building blocks or stones), or to support or protect other yard elements (composting bin enclosure).

2.4.3. Yard Size
Yard size varies with several factors:

- *Population density.* Yards tend to increase in size from urban to suburban and rural areas.
- *History.* Urban yards in newer neighborhoods or residential blocks with newer houses tend to be smaller than those in older neighborhoods or ones where land has been less subdivided.
- *House size.* The larger the house on a given plot, the smaller the yard.
- *Money.* More of it can buy a larger yard.

Other factors are market supply, zoning, and urban planning.

The yardwork guerrilla learns at the outset of his struggle the square footage of his yard and its dimensions. He plots the measurements on the lot map obtained from the city for future reference and planning. The dimensions of the battlefield inform his thinking about the magnitude of the transformation he envisions and the actions required to achieve it; the bigger the yard, the more complex, involved, and time-consuming the war. Yard size also impacts needed financial outlays as well as the course, frequency, intensity, and type of attacks.

2.4.4. Yard Sections
Every yard typically consists of three areas defined based on their relationship to the house and the street:

- Front yard
- Side yard
- Back yard

The *front yard* lies between the dwelling and the street. There the yardwork guerrilla showcases and promotes his vision; there he manifests the revolutionary yard change he aims to affect. Being the most public area of any property, the front yard mostly serves decorative purposes, but the staunch yardwork insurgent makes little distinction between yard sections and uses the front yard to grow fruits and vegetables.

The front yard's exposure to neighbors and passersby brings both advantages and disadvantages. On the one hand, by being seen the yardwork guerrilla can gain a great deal of goodwill and admiration for his hard work. Even a casual passerby can rarely resist commenting on the front yard's appearance to cultivate good relations. On the other hand, exposure imposes upon the G.Y. a degree of self-censorship.

The *side yard* stretches from the front yard along one or both sides of the dwelling, connecting the front to

"Front and back follow one another."
−Lao Tsu

the *back yard*, which extends from the rear face of the dwelling to the rear property line. Hidden from street view by the house and boundary barriers, the back yard offers privacy and operational security. The yardwork guerrilla prefers the back to be larger in area than the front yard.

2.4.5. Yard Terrain

In assessing the yard's terrain, a strategically important aspect of yard topography, the first task of the guerrilla yardworker is to establish landmarks: What principal features of the terrain give the yard its character? Landmarks anchor the insurgent's mental map of the yard the insurgent. Like an explorer, he fills in the blanks as he learns more about the yard. He

- adds high and low points, slope, wide plains and narrow spots, the far and the near;
- notes the land's unevenness and irregularities;
- distinguishes sunny spots, areas in partial shade, places in shade and under tree cover;
- separates areas under water from the land mass; and
- marks the built environment of the house, patio, and fence in opposition to the natural world.

The yardvolutionary updates his mental map of the yard as a battlefield following each battle (see 5.1.4. Draw Maps).

The most favorable terrain for guerrilla yardwork is *flat land*. The flat yard offers maximum ease of access, clear sight lines, and the least amount of operational effort. The *sloping yard* presents various challenges, depending on the slope's direction and grade. The yard's slope may be partial, as when one or more flat sections or portions of the yard lead up to or extend down from a slope. The slope may ascend (slope up) or descend (slope down) from the dwelling's front, side, or rear. If the house sits on a slope, typically the front yard descends from the house and the back yard ascends. Several combinations of slope direction and location are possible. The G.Y. generally prefers to proceed upward and with the house at his back.

The yard's terrain can feature a variety of natural or artificial surfaces. Dirt is like a blank canvas on which the yardwork guerrilla can paint the revolution. The yard's terrain tends to already be covered with various elements. Of these, the lawn remains the most widespread: its aesthetic and recreational functions make the lawn a typical home and yard owner's darling, and its cultural aspect as a symbol of affluence and 'Americanness' cannot be denied. Solid patches of grass can appear to be the easiest to maintain: at the first glance the lawn only requires regular mowing and watering. However, the lawn presents a distinct set of challenges. It wastes space, particularly for the urban farmer and G.Y. with a small yard. It drains energy and material. Keeping the lawn weed-free requires extra effort, including fertilizing, weeding, and reseeding, as well as water and chemicals. The negative environmental impact of the lawn far outweighs any of its positives. If the G.Y. wishes to replace the lawn with other yard elements, he finds it an especially difficult opponent. The lawn grows from a tough layer of sod several inches thick; the older the lawn, the more settled and tougher the sod as the grass root system, foot traffic, and the elements solidified the layer.

"The [yardwork] guerrilla's best ally is the terrain and because this is so he must know it like the palm of his hand."
—Carlos Marighella, re-interpreted

The G.Y. must remove the sod clumps, either by hauling them away or piling them, grass down/dirt up, in a different area of the yard. Because the removal of sod lowers elevation by a few inches, the G.Y. must replace the dirt, and, finally, cover it with a layer of bark dust or chips (the yardwork guerrilla leaves no area with exposed soil).

Mulching entails covering the lawn with a thick layer of bark mulch, straw, chopped leaves, grass clippings, or sawdust. In a layered approach newspapers or cardboard provide the base layer and organic materials the top one. Aside from saving the effort digging up the lawn sod, mulching suppresses weeds and helps retain moisture. Organic materials provide nutrients for the soil.

Other natural yard surfaces include areas covered with plants, shrubs, bushes, or trees; rocky or sandy areas; bodies of water, such as ponds or lakes; or waterways, such as brooks, creeks, and other streams. Human-made surfaces include stepping stones, pavers, bricks, and decorative rocks, all of which require special maintenance.

2.4.6. Vertical Yard

The vertical dimension, often overlooked in yard assessments, can be used to maximize space, particularly in smaller yards. Going vertical increases the yardvolution's area (see 2.4.7. Yard Elements). For example, food can come from all kinds of plants:

- *Ground*: beets, carrots, potatoes
- *Ground covers*: juniper, strawberry, thyme
- *Annuals*: lettuce, pea, tomato
- *Perennials*: asparagus, mint, rhubarb
- *Vines*: grapes, hops, kiwis
- *Shrubs*: currants, elderberries, raspberries
- *Trees*: fruit and nut trees come in various sizes and can thus further subdivide the vertical yard space

In considering the yard's verticality, the G.Y. must also keep in mind vantage points and sun exposure. As a general rule, smaller plants should be in front of taller ones so that all can be seen and all receive the right amount of sunlight.

Fig. 2 "When the forces of oppression come to maintain themselves in power against established law, peace is considered already broken."

2.4.7. Yard Elements

Elements of the yard can be classified in three ways. First, the first-time home and yard owner discovers some elements upon purchase and others he creates in the course of ownership.

Yard elements can be human-made or built, and natural. Nothing grows in areas occupied by *human-made elements*, which can include a tool shed, a patio, paths or stepping stones, a detached hot tub, a chicken coop, a fire pit, or any seating placed directly on the ground. A deck or porch attached to the house extends the built area. Planter boxes feature human-made walls enclosing a dirt mass, which renders them a cross-over element. Human-made areas require construction and regular maintenance.

Natural yard elements include trees, bushes, shrubs, grasses, flowers, and vegetable plants. More rare are streams and bodies of standing water. Because of their renewable character, natural yard elements require constant care and cultivation, albeit aided by Nature.

Yard elements can also be divided by use or function. *Utilitarian elements* have a productive function and include elements dedicated to growing food, including fruits, vegetables, and herbs. Fruit trees, vegetable patches, or planter boxes serve this purpose best. Food-related utilitarian elements tend to require the most attention and the least room for tactical improvisation. Certain vegetable plants, for example, may need watering, thinning, aeration, or trimming at particular times in order to yield their bounty. Utilitarian areas that require less upkeep include the shed, the compost pile or bin, and the yard-waste pile.

Recreational elements serve the yardwork guerrilla as places of rest, respite, and relaxation. Here is where he spends time in between engagements, gathering strength, collecting thoughts, and hatching plans. Here is where he can also escape from the responsibilities of his struggle; paradoxically, the guerrilla yardwork can best hide from the demands of the yard revolution right on the battlefield. Recreational elements require most effort on the front end—in construction, assembly, purchase, or planting. They include a patio, a barbecue area, a fire pit, a hammock, chairs or benches, fragrant plants (lilac, jasmine, lavender, or roses), or trees. Larger trees provide opportunities for climbing to obtain an aerial view of the battlefield; tree shade offers an extremely valuable recreational benefit as well.

Decorative elements provide visual delight; their balance and harmony with Nature caresses the eye and nourishes well-being. The yardwork guerrilla strives to emulate the natural environment of his climate zone primarily through decorative yard elements, including trees, shrubs, ornamental grasses, rocks, walls, water features (pond, waterfall, stream), sculptures, and areas covered by bark mulch or small rocks.

A narrow passage providing access to and from various areas and elements, the path combines the three functions. A multitude of materials can be used to build paths, all of which require a different degree and type of maintenance: bark chips, gravel, stone, bricks, concrete chunks, and even succulent ground covers.

2.5. Operations Base

Even though all the guerrilla yardwork struggle takes place in the yard, the house must feature prominently in every battle plan as the base of operations. First, the possession of the house births the possibility of yardvolution (see 4.1. Objective Conditions for Guerrilla Yardwork). All action radiates from the house; all action revolves around it. As the revolutionary's base camp, the house constitutes a natural center and reference

```
"Beauty is truth,
 truth beauty, that
 is all
 Ye know on earth, and
 all ye need to know."
 -John Keats
```

point of the revolutionary yard war. The insurgent begins each battle there and she returns there afterward to rest, train, watch television, admire her progress, and plan her next move. During battle, the house must be at her back as much as possible to provide physical and psychological security for action.

The house provides the following operational functions:

- Housing
- Messing
- Planning
- Briefing and debriefing
- Training
- Medical and dispensary service
- Rest
- Storage and stockpiling
- Morale services
- Receiving
- Staging of detachments
- Communication
- Intelligence gathering and disseminating

Several characteristics of the house impact the yardvolution's course. Dwelling type will affect the yard's shape and area. A single-family dwelling typically features a yard on all its four sides, with the front and back being the largest. A duplex will have the yard on three sides, while a townhouse a narrow yard in the front and back. Narrow and long, a mobile home creates a sizeable side yard and smaller front and backyard areas. Mobile home parks rarely use fences to divide lots, which can create boundary disputes the yardwork guerrilla must avoid at all cost.

The position of the house on the property affects the size and shape of yard sections:

- A house located *close to the front of the lot* creates a larger back yard. Greater privacy enhances operational freedom and flexibility, making this option preferable.
- A house positioned *close to the rear boundary* creates a larger front yard. Most of guerrilla yardwork must be conducted in public view.
- A house *in the corner of the lot* creates a large side yard and, depending on the corner, eliminates the front or back yard. The resulting L-shape offers interesting possibilities, though the house obstructs some sight lines.
- A house positioned *in the center of the lot* creates a front, a back, and two side yards that are roughly equal in size. It also obstructs sight lines in each section.

"A guerrilla base may be defined as an area, strategically located, in which the guerrillas can carry out their duties of training, self-preservation, and development."
–Mao Tse Tung

Unless it explodes due to a gas leak or gets leveled by a runaway truck, for example, the house as the operations base offers a solid, friendly structure the G.Y. can rely on for safety and shelter. Mostly good things come out of the house, such as troop support or calls for refreshments. By contrast, with the fence at her back the guerrilla exposes herself to surprise attacks by neighbors, children, ground animals, birds, or rogue traffic.

2.6. Strategic Yard Areas

In addition to physical sections, yards can be classified from the strategic standpoint. The most famous strategic classification comes from Sun Tzu:

- In the *ground of dissolution* Bad and Good Nature fight with vigor. The yardwork guerrilla must resolve the resulting thicket by removing or trimming plants.
- Nearest to the house, *light ground* provides access routes to more remote areas.
- The *ground of contention* covers most of the yard. Controlling it would be advantageous to both sides.
- Both the yardwork guerrilla and non-combatants can access *trafficked ground*, including the right of way outside the property's boundary.
- *Intersecting ground* is surrounded on three sides by neighbors. It, therefore, requires building alliances more than any other ground.
- *Heavy ground* abuts property boundaries from the outside, requiring occasional entry to retrieve items, repair the fence, or access outward-facing yard elements.
- *Bad ground* is difficult to access. The guerrilla generally avoids purchasing land that includes bad ground, including rocky terrain, marsh, or landslide.
- Narrow and enclosed, *surrounded ground* requires a circuitous way in and out. It includes corners and areas behind structures.
- *Dying ground* includes land where the G.Y. can injure herself or perish, including areas under a tree or branch close to falling; a hole from a stump, excavation, or an old well; or soil covering unexploded ordnance.

Another classification divides yard mass by level of control.

- *Areas under enemy control* include yard portions where the G.Y. has yet to put her stamp—Bad Nature reigns here. Over the course of the yardvolution, the area under enemy control diminishes to zero as the area under the guerrilla's control expands to the entire property.

- *Areas under the yardwork guerrilla's control* have undergone revolutionary transformation. Area superiority offers the insurgent temporary control of the area, attained through maximum use of surprise and maneuver and offering a period of time to accomplish missions without prohibitive interference by enemy. The G.Y. aims for area supremacy, i.e. complete control over the area so that Bad Nature lacks ways to effectively interfere with his operations.

> "So it is that good warriors take their stand on ground where they cannot lose."
> -Sun Tzu

- *Twilight zone areas* are located between areas of enemy control and temporary guerrilla control. The G.Y. and Bad Nature compete for overt control of the twilight zone. Guerrilla yardwork requires operating on Bad Nature's flanks, where She is at Her weakest, especially in areas bordering those under the insurgent's control.

2.7. Recognizing Guerrilla Yards

Guerrilla yardwork relies on stealth and surprise. Unless on a propaganda or recruitment mission, the guerrilla yardworker never reveals his identity as such or discloses his involvement in the yardvolution. Instead, he lets the results of his battles speak for themselves. Yards transformed by guerrilla yardwork manifest several commonalities:

- *Natural appearance.* The yardvolution emulates Nature both in method and appearance. Yard elements are placed in unpredictable and seemingly random locations, without appearing to conform to any master plan. No patterns, such as rows or shapes, can be discerned.

Many different plants grow without hindrance, save for occasional pruning or replanting when the enemy begins to encroach. The natural appearance reflects the yardwork guerrilla's relaxed, creative character.

- *Unfinished look.* Nature is never finished and neither is guerrilla yardwork. Constant activity belongs to guerrilla yardworker's arsenal. The yard reflects this ever-changing situation. Guerrilla yardwork's focus on small battles and on small areas results in the yard being in-between one battle or another at all times. Because the guerrilla yardworker occasionally allows weeds to grow and desired plants to get out of control, some describe the unfinished look as unkempt.

- *Relaxed feel.* Many home and yard owners express their need for control by creating straight lines, neat edges, weed-free lawns, precision-trimmed shrubs, and other features of the manicured look. This presents the impression of untouchability. By contrast, the yard transformed by guerrilla yardwork invites interaction—it asks to be touched, caressed, picked. It makes the owner and visitor alike comfortable at first sight. Where the manicured look resembles the strict parent, the yardvolutionary look is the beer buddy. The natural, unfinished appearance creates a loose, comfortable atmosphere.

A special case of a yardvolutionized urban area is the community garden, a publicly owned piece of land enclosed by a fence or other barrier and converted for collective gardening. While growing food tends to be the primary goal of community gardening, some community gardens focus specifically on propagating native plants or attracting wildlife to create habitat. Community gardening spurs social interaction. Because many community gardens consist of patches cultivated by different people, contact occurs on a frequent basis. Despite the absence of ownership, community gardens present fertile ground for guerrilla yardwork: different people gardening at different, unpredictable times in different, unknowable ways guarantees a relaxed, messy, and natural appearance.

2.8. Areas of Importance Beyond the Yard

Neither the yard as the theater of operations nor guerrilla yardwork as a method exist in a vacuum. The structure of space beyond the first-time home and yard owner's property comes into play during the planning and operational stages of the yardvolutionary struggle.

2.8.1. Neighboring Yards

The G.Y.'s relationship between her and her neighbors' yards, both in terms of spatial organization and aesthetic continuity, provides a long-term context and crucial strategic backdrop to the yardvolutionary struggle. The yard may be the insurgent's exclusive domain, but it's preferable to wage the revolution amongst friendly forces.

The yardwork guerrilla's area of influence is her yard; her area of interest also includes nearby properties. The G.Y. must obtain basic familiarity with the yards of all immediate neighbors and the neighbors across the street from her and her immediate neighbors' properties. Over time, she works outward to other yards and their owners. The methods of reconnaissance include observation from her home's windows, across the fence from her yard, and from the street; personal visits, e.g. during house or block parties; and reports from such observation and visits by her spouse or other family members. Aerial views from satellite images available on online mapping websites can also be helpful.

The yardwork guerrilla uses intelligence about the neighboring yards to assess the character of their owners, anticipate their actions in relation to her effort, and acquire inspiration for the appearance of and actions in her yard. In addition to such outside-in information flow, the yardwork guerrilla works every day to turn neighboring yards into territories positively disposed to her vision and makes every effort to export the yardvolution beyond her yard's boundary (see 5.5.2. Propaganda).

2.8.2. Street and Neighborhood

Street traffic, which includes pedestrians, and motorized and non-motorized vehicles poses a special set of challenges. A quiet street, with little foot or vehicular traffic, allows the yardwork guerrilla to proceed with greater freedom from observation than a busy street where watchful eyes of passersby, bicyclists, and drivers put her under greater scrutiny. Even a moderately trafficked street brings additional problems, such as litter, dog excrement and a higher likelihood of theft, vandalism, or trespassing. Streets with higher traffic volumes also generate more noise and air pollution. Proximity to busy streets or shopping areas increases the likelihood of these drawbacks occurring.

"[T]he guerrilla fighter needs to have a good knowledge of the surrounding countryside, the paths of entry and escape, the possibilities of speedy maneuver, good hiding places; naturally also, he must count on the support of the people."
–Che Guevara

To determine her neighborhood's character the home and yard owner conducts online research and reconnaissance on foot, on bike, or by car. She first explores her block, then the wider neighborhood, to gradually acquire intimate knowledge of her zone. Familiarity with the neighborhood informs her about the aesthetic standards prevailing in the area, characteristics of the people living in the neighborhood, and shopping options.

2.9. Constitution of Yard Space

Rather than by its size, the yard should be viewed for its transformational potential; the yard is a territory of a new order. As an agent of social and environmental change, the guerrilla yardworker transforms her yard, creating a home for herself and her family. In turn, the insurgent's progress depends on the characteristics of the space she aims to transform. The yard, therefore, results from her actions and structures them at the same time.

"The task of revolutionary forces in each [yard] is to initiate the struggle when the conditions are present there, regardless of the conditions in other [yards]."
–Che Guevara, reinterpreted

The smart yardwork guerrilla maps both her ultimate vision and intermediate stages to mark her progress. The maps feature the outlines of the yard and house boundaries, yard elements and areas, including paths and other access routes, and indications of plants. A comparison of the maps sketched in the course of the struggle, perhaps on an annual basis, can serve as a powerful motivational tool on the path to victory.

When personalizing their yards many property owners follow examples of other yards from magazines or websites (HGTV.com alone lists no fewer than 17 styles of outdoor spaces). Others aim to conform to various established philosophies or principles of spatial organization, such as feng shui. The yardwork guerrilla views such examples as inspiration at best. Guerrilla yardwork does not prescribe the yard's appearance beyond simple guidelines (see 2.7. Recognizing Guerrilla

Yards). Rather than conform to arbitrary standards or practices, the yardwork insurgent constructs her own reality and manifests her own personal vision through guerrilla yardwork.

A similar principle applies to guerrilla yardwork as a method. Many property owners rely on advice from television shows, books, or magazines. A true yardwork guerrilla uses Nature's constraints, such as the climate zone or growing season, to her advantage. While many of her actions approximate advice of 'gardening experts,' the yardwork guerrilla finds greatest achievement in discovering the best course of action for herself.

To a degree, the yard as a combination of structural pieces determines the guerrilla's decisions about her actions. Every yard configuration influences the range and selection of guerrilla tactics. Conversely, during the yardvolutionary struggle the insurgent alters the yard's structural dimension to realize her vision. She works to create the yard of her dreams; her vision results from different sets of actions, which include

- *Combat (formation)*: digging, removal, planting, construction
- *Governing (maintenance)*: mowing, pruning, trimming, weeding, watering
- *Enjoyment (intended use)*: recreation, harvest

These sets of actions change the yard as a structure over time. Thanks to guerrilla yardwork, the position of each structural element, relationships between them, and the overall appearance and utility of the yard evolve. In the interplay between the yard as a structure and the guerrilla yardworker's actions altering the structure, the yard becomes constituted as a space. The development of this spatial constitution comprises revolutionary yard change. Three stages can be distinguished:

- *Initial*: the yard as the yardwork guerrilla finds it upon the purchase of the property.
- *Transitional*: the succession of structural configurations resulting from guerrilla yardworker's actions over time. Each action she takes creates a different configuration, and in struggling to achieve the final stage she may go through numerous structural combinations. The transitional stage is the longest.
- *Final*: the realized vision of the home and yard owner. At the same time, the yardwork guerrilla realizes that her struggle has no end. Once she becomes a yardwork guerrilla, she will remain a yardwork guerrilla. Moreover, Bad Nature's reactionary forces attempt counter-revolution on a daily basis, fighting to overturn the G.Y.'s achievements. Guerrilla yardwork is for life.

3

Combatants

In a protracted conflict with Bad Nature the guerrilla yard-worker struggles to transform the portion of Earth's surface in his possession. Various non-combatants accompany him on the yardvolutionary path, some aiding and others hampering his struggle at various places and times.

3.1. Guerrilla Yardworker: Yard Reformer

Who is the yardwork guerrilla? Every G.Y. exhibits common traits, discernible with a naked eye through conversation, in action, or with the aid of documentation and statistical evidence. Subjective characteristics remain hidden or only manifest themselves over a long period of time.

3.1.1. Objective Characteristics of the Yardwork Guerrilla

This *Handbook* considers the first-time home and yard owner to be within five to seven years of the purchase of his first real estate property and during the major yard improvement operations. The novelty of the ownership experience dissipates as the obligations of mortgage payments and child rearing usurp his attention. The toughest battles take place at the outset. The struggle itself typically lasts only a few years: most major projects tend to be completed within five to seven years of ownership (yard transformation proceeds in parallel to home improvement). Like children, as plants mature they require less attention. Similarly, as major projects are completed, the G.Y. runs out of room for transformation and must redirect his focus to maintenance and repair.

Demographic Profile

The typical yardwork guerrilla is a first-time home and yard owner in a city or a town (see 2.3. Relationship to City). His median age is 31; most first-time home and yard owners are between 25 and 35 years of age (by contrast, the median repeat buyer is 53 years old). In this period, most people begin to settle down, switch from jobs into careers, and start procreating. This is also the age of peak physical form and of coming into one's own as an individual (30 has been colloquially described as the 'hump of adulthood').

"The best age for a guerrilla fighter varies between 25 and 35 years, a stage in which the life of most persons has assumed a definite shape."
–Che Guevara

In the year prior to the Great Recession of 2008-2009, about one half of first-time home and yard buyers were married couples and 11% were unmarried couples; in 2011 two thirds of first-time home and yard buyers made the home purchase as a couple (in recent years, the percentage of home and yard buyers who are couples, particularly married ones, has been on the increase as dual income better positions them to qualify for a mortgage). The rest of the first-timers are single: one in four is a single female and 11% are single males. The yardwork guerrilla fights with support from a spouse or partner.

The median income of a first-time home and yard buyer in 2011 was $62,400, up from $59,900 in 2010. First-timers

Fig. 3 "Guerrilla [yardwork] is a pledge the guerrilla makes to himself."

purchase smaller and less expensive homes and yards than repeat buyers: on average, a 1,570 square-foot home costing $155,000, compared to the repeat buyer's 2,100 square-foot home costing $219,500 (on a $96,600 annual income). It can be safely assumed that a smaller square footage of the home correlates with a smaller acreage of the adjacent yard. The vanguard of the yardvolution is a medium-income American who fights on a small territory.

The G.Y. is a middle-class individual, with a college degree, and some post-college job experience. He likely believes in the long-term value of home and yard ownership or, like 60% of all first-time buyers, wishes to purchase a home out of a simple desire to own a home of his own—attitudes that signify the maturity and values of adulthood. Despite beginning to hold many values of middle age, with the onset of the 30's he also realizes the limitations of adulthood. Children, if any, are objects of unconditional love, albeit at the cost of a massive strain on resources. Though his parents and in-laws may have helped with a down payment and may even continue assisting financially after the purchase (see 1.1.4. Heed Others' Expectations), the expectation increases for him to make his own way.

"As long as a person is willing to fight, his social condition or position is no consideration, but only men who are courageous and determined can bear the hardships of guerrilla campaigning in a protracted war."
—Mao Tse-Tung

Whether he holds a white or a green or a blue collar job, the climb up an organizational or a career ladder increases demands on time spent at the workplace. Except when his job constitutes an extension of his life's passion, which is rare, wage labor becomes instrumental, rather than expressive—a revenue source and a means to various ends, including the ownership of the home and yard, rather than an extension of self. He remembers having cultivated creative pursuits like writing, music, or painting in younger age, and abandoning them under the pressures of adulthood. The desire intensifies to resume such old or take up new hobbies, as does the need to cultivate relationships with the spouse or partner, friends, and family. Consequently, the value of time skyrockets.

Mornings, evenings, weekends, and vacation days become precious, not to be wasted. Largely due to the general shortage of spare time, guerrilla yardwork emerges as a viable option for transforming the first-time home and yard owner's property.

An average American will own more than one home and yard in his lifetime but only the ownership of the first one tends to lend itself to guerrilla yardwork. Many of the demographic and personal characteristics of the first-time home and yard owner changed during and following the Great Recession of 2008-2009. For example, with tighter credit for mortgage loans and more strained incomes, by 2011 not only did the number and proportion of first-time home and yard owners decrease, they have been waiting longer to make the purchase and appear to be less likely to move quickly.

3.2. Subjective Qualities of the Yardwork Guerrilla

Objective characteristics describe the guerrilla yardworker, but in and of themselves they do not make her. The G.Y. possesses and exhibits several important internal qualities.

3.2.1. Knowledge of Self

The yardwork guerrilla's character must be apparent to her fellow fighters, people in her circle, and the population of the zone at large. She can only lead the yardvolution by outwardly manifesting the characteristics of the vanguard. To do so, she must possess keen awareness of such qualities: only by knowing herself can she show others who she is and what she is fighting to achieve. Otherwise she will fail, second-guessing herself in the heat of battle, faltering in her resolve at a crucial moment, or retreating into a shell of self-doubt when the going gets tough.

"Knowing the self is enlightenment."
-Lao Tsu

"So it is said that if you know others and know yourself, you will not be imperiled in a hundred battles."
-Sun Tzu

The G.Y. must know her qualities, proclivities, and habits from the outset. Every battle changes both the yard and the guerrilla; as her body, skills, and resolve harden, her qualities evolve. Hence she must continually assess her state of mind, physical shape, and identification with purpose. The foundation of self-reflection and the outlook of self-improvement aid the guerrilla in meeting every task with calm and resolve.

3.2.2. Revolutionary Consciousness

To embark on the guerrilla yardwork path, the home and yard owner must possess a distinct consciousness of the necessity of change—a necessary condition for any yardvolution. Before he transforms himself into the yardwork guerrilla, the first-time home and yard owner must gain awareness that the yard needs to be altered in some way, whether in appearance, functionality, or both. Without this awareness, status quo persists. Particularly in the early stages of the yardvolution, when the thrill of struggle and its possibilities reverberates through the new insurgent, he can pass judgments on the masses whose revolutionary consciousness has yet to form. Every G.Y. has the responsibility to assist his fellow men and women in stepping onto the revolutionary path (see 3.3.3. Recruitment).

Revolutionary consciousness can develop in various ways and over different periods of time. Its foundation is laid when the first-time home and yard owner assesses the condition of the yard and identifies a difference between its current state and what he sees in his (or his spouse's) mind's eye. He can start transforming himself into the yardwork guerrilla the moment he sets down his beer, puts on a pair of work gloves, and grasps the handle of a shovel; the moment he gets off the couch during the half-time show and fires up the weed whacker; or the moment he realizes his midnight snack is missing a cherry tomato that could be ripening on the back-yard vine. In such cases, the purpose and methods of guerrilla yardwork will develop later, either with the assistance of this *Handbook* or with help from more experienced yardwork guerrillas. The advantage of this approach to developing yardvolutionary consciousness is its speed and flexibility: no time gets wasted starting the revolution and the yardwork guerrilla can adapt on the go. On the other hand, the trial-and-error method can be time-consuming and squander valuable resources.

"When you take your arms in hand, you become soldiers."
-Mao Tse-Tung

Revolutionary consciousness may also emerge from conducting yardwork in a regular fashion. A lack of progress in his yard travails may discourage the cash-strapped and time-pressured first-time property owner, forcing him to wonder whether there is another way. He may search for resources online or talk to friends or neighbors, discover the *Handbook*, and change course right away. The conversion from regular to guerrilla yardwork is perhaps the most powerful way of acquiring revolutionary consciousness. Direct experience of the two methods allows for easy comparison of benefits.

Alternatively, the first-time home and yard owner can first read this *Handbook* and acquire revolutionary consciousness through advance study. As he learns more about the various facets of the guerrilla yardwork method, he finds it exceedingly suitable for his yard and matching his principles. The study approach leads to greater preparedness, which strongly correlates with success in battle, and to faster, more systematic progress once the yard revolution commences. On the flip side, advance learning delays the start of the yardvolution.

Another path to revolutionary consciousness is peer influence. An experienced friend or an acquaintance can introduce the first-time home and yard owner to guerrilla yardwork. The friend may deliberately recruit fellow home and yard owners. A casual conversation about the trials and tribulations of home and yard ownership can lead to the discussion of guerrilla yardwork as an alternative. The home and yard owner may also discover guerrilla yardwork through propaganda by insurgents in his or other communities (see 5.5.2. Propaganda).

Continuing and completing the yardvolution requires that revolutionary consciousness be cultivated. The yardwork guerrilla can keep the revolutionary spirit alive in many ways:

- Enjoy the fruits of victory after each battle.
- Consume produce from the garden at his table or share it with others.
- Host events, e.g. garden parties or BBQ's, in his yard.
- Receive moral support, encouragement, and practical advice from fellow troops.
- Recruit new yardvolutionaries.
- Mentor a new or less experienced insurgent.
- Engage in propaganda efforts.
- Re-read the *Handbook* or buy a new copy to replace a tattered original.
- Give copies of the *Handbook* to friends and family.

In addition to cultivating the consciousness of the necessity of change, the incipient guerrilla yardworker must also believe such revolutionary change is possible. He must believe not only that the yard *must* be transformed but also that it *can* be transformed. He must also trust that he can execute the transformation. These beliefs give the yardwork guerrilla the will to fight and lend him the ingredients for developing a sense of purpose for his struggle.

The insurgent must also be open to change within himself. Improvements in physique may pry the mind's door open, but only complete openness to changes in his thinking can render guerrilla yardwork effective.

The transformation into a yardwork guerrilla brings challenges. Methodical individuals may resist the method's seeming randomness; devil-may-care individuals may struggle with clear outlines of the method's principles. Conservatives may find the revolutionary aspect of guerrilla yardwork hard to swallow; liberals may find dissatisfaction with the slow pace of change. People with sedentary jobs or lifestyles may hurt from the war's physical demands; active people may suffer from being tied down to a single locale or from adjusting to a new range of movements. The personal transition into a yardvolutionary means overcoming obstacles, but once the process gets well under way, the new yardwork guerrilla never looks back.

3.2.3. Character of the Yardwork Guerrilla

Guerrilla yardwork requires a certain sort of individual. Ideally the G.Y. possesses necessary qualities at the outset, but the yardvolution's progress can aid in cultivating those qualities in later stages of the struggle.

The yardwork guerrilla must possess great powers of endurance, which runs on the fuel of self-discipline. Persistence to the point of stubbornness prevents flight and surrender. To persevere in a protracted conflict, the yardvolution insurgent must display physical and mental fortitude (see 5.5.1. Cultivation of Health). The yardwork guerrilla must also retain a clear order of life priorities and focus on the efficient execution of each. She must eliminate all distractions that sap her energy, and stay vigilant for diversions. She must also reserve time for rest (see 5.4. Rest).

The guerrilla yardworker is a person of action. In accordance with the basic tenets of guerrilla yardwork strategy, she is always on the offensive, retaining initiative and surprise (see 4.2. The Strategy of Guerrilla Yardwork). Except to keep within the attack-withdrawal-attack cycle of action, she never retreats. Such a proactive outlook requires fearlessness as well as patience. The G.Y. prefers to make mistakes doing something rather doing nothing for fear of mistakes. She is unafraid of failure, real or perceived, and does not get discouraged by erring. Instead, she learns from her missteps.

The insurgent must seek knowledge, both about herself and about her enemy. New intelligence, tactics, and circumstances all generate new information that needs to be digested and incorporated into battle planning and action. The yardwork guerrilla must be as hungry for knowledge as she is for the food she's growing, so that she can achieve more with less effort and resources. She must be cunning and capable of swift comprehension and inventiveness in order to adapt to circumstances. Imagination and creativity take a central position in striving for self-reliance and self-sufficiency; versatility comes closely behind.

> "This fighting attitude, this attitude of not being dismayed at any time, this inflexibility when confronting the great problems in the final objective is also the nobility of the guerrilla fighter. To the stoicism imposed by the difficult conditions of warfare should be added an austerity born of rigid self-control that will prevent a single excess, a single slip, whatever the circumstances. The guerrilla soldier should be an ascetic."
> –Che Guevara

The guerrilla yardworker must also be a brave and positive individual. Her astuteness must compensate for her deficiencies in arms and equipment. To prevail over Bad Nature, she must summon all her strength and courage. She must be capable of fending off detractors from her circles, declining invitations to barbecues or hikes when she is planning a strike, and avoiding other social obligations when she wavers in her willingness to fight. Her audacity and resolve will help her prevail in battle. At all times the G.Y. must be prepared to face the changing circumstances with a positive outlook, if not optimism. She knows she is unstoppable.

> "[T]he guerrilla fighter, as a person conscious of a role in the vanguard of the people, must have a moral conduct that shows him to be a true priest of the reform to which he aspires."
> –Che Guevara

Qualities that complement the basic set of personal traits pertaining to inner strength include idealism, aesthetic sensibility, and love of Nature. Practical combat skills include spatial awareness, basic understanding of topography, as well as the ability to measure and calculate distances, determine routes, and draw maps, plans, and schedules.

3.3. The Yardvolutionary Army

Though the yardwork guerrilla fights alone in his yard, he has company in yards all around the country. The guerrilla yardwork army comprises all individual yardvolutionaries, loosely organized in self-perpetuating bands.

3.3.1. The Size of the Yardvolutionary Army
How many yardwork guerrillas are there? Due to the stealth nature of the yardvolutionary struggle and a lack of statistical

evidence, the strength of the guerrilla yardwork army can only be estimated with indirect measures.

Thirty-seven percent of all home and yard buyers in 2011 were novices (down from 50% in 2010, a sign of continued tight mortgage credit). Half of all homes were purchased in suburbs, 18% in urban areas, 18% in small towns, and 11% in rural areas. Not only do suburban areas have a higher supply of residences, they attract people who either lived there already (the median distance from a previous residence is 12 miles) or are moving there to start or continue growing a family. It is safe to assume that first-time home and yard owners in urban areas constitute a minority among home and yard owners. Let us assume that less than one fifth of all first-time home and yard buyers are potential guerrilla yardworkers.

Extrapolating based on the number of homes purchased in 2011, first-time home buyers totaled approximately 1.9 million individuals. Urban first-timers numbered some 342,000 individuals. The ranks of potential yardwork guerrillas swell every year as more Americans purchase their homes. Even with the lower percentage of first-timers in 2011, multiplying that year's figures by 6 (the average duration of the guerrilla yard revolution) yields more than 2 million people. At any moment the pool of the guerrilla army potentially exceeds the combined total of U.S. active and reserve duty military personnel. The greater the number of people who read and adopt this *Handbook*, the stronger the guerrilla army.

"[The] guerrilla band is an armed nucleus, the fighting vanguard of the people."
-Che Guevara

"The more such bands there are, the better will the situation be."
-Mao Tse-Tung

3.3.2. The Organization of the Yardvolutionary Army
Critics posit that the vast sea of yardwork guerrillas conducting private revolutions in their yards comprises an undifferenti-

ated mass of individuals, acting on their own accord. Lack of organization or concerted effort allegedly precludes considering yardvolutionaries as anything but men and women landscaping their properties, akin to the mass of people watching television or making meals for their families. The yardvolutionary retorts with two facts. First, the common goal, purpose, and strategy unite the agents of each individual yardvolution into a nationwide armed movement of kindred spirits working to change the world. Secondly, aided by community life and online communication, guerrilla yardworkers often organize into loose units to facilitate progress in their yards.

"While [guerrilla units] function as guerrillas, they may be compared to innumerable fleas, which, by biting a giant both in front and in rear, ultimately exhaust him."
-Mao Tse-Tung

In his yard the guerrilla yardworker tends to act alone. Beyond it, he's part of a decentralized network of guerrilla yardworkers. On the national scale, the men and women who are lone wolves in their yards constitute an army. Dispersed as they are from shining sea to sea, the common enemy links them into a powerful force. The tie that binds them is difficult, if not impossible to destroy: the unifying philosophy and practice of guerrilla yardwork provides a bond that only wealth and death may sever. The yardwork guerrilla may work alone in his yard, but he has company in his struggle.

Yardwork guerrillas organize both online and offline. Personal knowledge of more than a handful of fellow yardvolutionaries may not be necessary for success. The solitary nature of the guerrilla's labor finds a powerful counterpart in the online network of fighters sharing common goals. The Internet constitutes a strategic hinterland for insurgents where they can connect, communicate, and socialize with one other. It is also the one place where Bad Nature cannot encroach. The ever-growing pool of shared resources and communication provides guerrilla yardworkers with a virtual base of psychological and moral support, a respite for rest and inspiration, and a platform for the exchange of practical advice and other intelligence. Whether it's the blog at GuerrillaYardwork.com, the Guerrilla Yardwork Facebook page, listservs, email newsletters, chat groups, or email, the Internet enables the guerrilla yardwork army to reinforce the sense of camaraderie, strength, and power that emerges in large groups fighting for a shared cause. The Internet also allows

"Unorganized guerrilla warfare cannot contribute to victory."
–Mao Tse-Tung

for recruiting new yardvolutionaries and publicizing the cause to the outside population (see 3.3.3. Recruitment and 5.5.2. Propaganda). Needless to say, the amount of time spent online should never exceed the amount of time spent in the yard (see 1.3.3. Reclaim the Self).

Online social networking enables yardwork guerrillas to connect in person. Particularly if they live in close proximity, e.g. the same block or street or neighborhood, personal connections with other yardvolutionaries can strengthen them as fighters. They may assemble for occasional gatherings in pubs or each other's yards to commiserate or exchange tactical tips. Over time they may form more distinctive bands that percolate through the urban environment like rainwater through the ground (see 5.5.3. Communication and Social Networking).

A more traditional way to meet fellow guerrilla yardwork fighters is at house or garden parties or to approach them after detecting a yard that appears to be undergoing or a result of a yard revolution (see 2.7. Recognizing Guerrilla Yards).

While yardvolutionary combat takes place on the individual level, the insurgency as a movement aggregates dispersed actions of each individual G.Y., orchestrating their effects into strategically significant advances against Bad Nature as a whole. Though guerrillas may communicate, exchange tips, or publicize their successes through a variety of channels, no pre-existing formal organization, leadership, or coordination exists among them. However, individual guerrilla yardworkers can spontaneously come together and organize informally and loosely for non-combat purposes. The extreme degree of autonomy on part of the individual guerrilla yardworker renders the organization not a command but a coordination-and-support structure. Organization of individual troops will differ from city to city, depending on the geographical layout, length and shape of blocks, number of properties on the block, and the demographic composition of the zone. In general, organization of the guerrilla yardwork army follows the country's administrative, geographical limits:

- *Squad (or squadron)*: a single block or a street up to 10 blocks in length, or a grouping of up to 10 blocks, all within a 10-minute walk from end to end
- *Platoon*: all squads within an officially designated neighborhood
- *Battalion*: all platoons within city limits (suburban columns may form an auxiliary brigade)
- *Brigade*: all battalions within a county
- *Division*: all brigades within a state
- *Army*: all brigades within the U.S. or other country's borders

"In guerrilla warfare, small units acting independently play the principal role. [T]hat most guerrilla troops are small makes it desirable and advantageous for them to appear and disappear in the enemy's rear. With such activities, the enemy is simply unable to cope. Because guerrilla formations act independently and because they are the most elementary of armed formations, command cannot be too highly centralized. If it were, guerrilla action would be too limited in scope."
-Mao Tse-Tung

The crucial as well as the most challenging level of organization is the squad. Disparate yardwork guerrillas may get to know their fellow fighters, but even a loose degree of organization requires effort. One of the yardvolutionaries in the zone must take it upon himself to lead the way and organize them. Thanks to the voluntary character of the struggle, others will likely follow suit, inspired by such an individual. Squad gatherings maintain neighborly character, with organization aiming to facilitate the lending and borrowing of power tools, exchange of tips and advice about tactics, tasks, and tools, and mutual acknowledgment of progress. Squad members may also gather to help with a fellow member's project, disperse, and gather again at another yard for another major project. Such collaborative attacks parallel the strategies of guerrilla yardwork on a greater scale.

Squadron leaders huddle with their counterparts to discuss platoon business, coordinate larger gatherings, or form tool libraries. Platoon leaders tackle citywide efforts and collaboration with the authorities and mission-aligned nonprofit organizations such as tree-planting groups or community gardens. Army leadership emerges from among platoon heads, with political guidance derived from the *Handbook*.

3.3.3. Recruitment

The primary way to grow the ranks of the yardwork guerrilla band is recruitment, an effort to convert uninitiated civilians into supporters, supporters into believers, and believers into actual warriors—no easy task. If the yardvolution is every guerrilla's responsibility, growing the ranks of the guerrilla yardwork army is her duty. A revolution can spread only if enough revolutionaries engage in it. A good G.Y. believes yards everywhere should be transformed through guerrilla yardwork, so she must work hard to grow the ranks of her comrades in tools.

The yardwork guerrilla's recruitment arsenal includes a number of powerful weapons:

- *The* Handbook. This is the simplest, most direct recruitment tool. Whether she loans her dog-eared copy or gives away extra new copies she has on hand—each method has its obvious pros and cons—she passes the book's wisdom on so that the reader may be persuaded straight from the source. As follow-up after a reasonable period of time, the G.Y. inquires about the recipient's opinion on the book, which, in turn, provides an easy opening salvo for discussion.

- *Conversation.* The G.Y. can describe her preferred method of yardwork in discussions with fellow home and yard owners.

- *Propaganda.* See 5.5.2. Propaganda.

- *The yard.* The yard's appearance can prompt passersby or members of her social circle to share words of appreciation, which creates an ideal opening for recruitment. Recognizing a yard resulting from guerrilla

> "The first task is to gain the absolute confidence of the inhabitants of the zone."
> –Che Guevara

> "The urban guerrilla must know how to live among the people and must be careful not to appear strange and separated from ordinary city life."
> –Carlos Marighella

yardwork can help the wavering home and yard owner to take the guerrilla yardwork path on her own property. It can help the devout yardwork guerrilla identify kindred spirits and form or join a cell of guerrilla yardworkers. It can help the dormant or retired insurgent rekindle the spirit of yard combat. Alternatively, the G.Y. can make herself visible and approachable to people in the zone while working in the yard, particularly its front section, and turn neighborly conversations about the yard's beauty to the promotion of the guerrilla method.

- *Leading by example.* While the *Handbook* constitutes the most tangible of recruitment tools, offering a rich fount of introductory information and pointing readers in the right direction, the yardwork guerrilla herself is the most effective one. She must make herself available as a resource to teach the method to whomever may be interested. She is a trusted advisor, always there to share encouraging words, offer suggestions, or lend a hand. The G.Y. leads by example, inspiring the masses, one by one, to rise and take up the tools of the yardvolution. Devouring a book may change the reader's perspective; befriending a leader transforms his life.

- *Work itself.* Another effective recruitment tool, useful also as an indoctrination and training method, is work itself—learning by doing. The first-time home and yard owner in the yardwork guerrilla's recruitment crosshairs must be persuaded to give the method a try, either in his own yard or helping in the recruiter's yard. Once the prospect grabs a shovel, he already walks the path leading to guerrilla yardwork (see 3.2.2. Revolutionary Consciousness). Guerrilla-style yardwork contains something intoxicating, even addictive: the lack of pressure, the physical invigoration, seeing the immediate results of one's effort, and capitalism-friendly philosophical underpinnings.

A combination of these methods can multiply the effects of the recruitment effort. The yardwork guerrilla can place in her front yard a brochure box containing flyers highlighting the yard's features and the method of creating them. She can wear the G.Y.-branded apparel while working in her yard or use it to spark conversations away from it. She can read the *Handbook* on public transportation, in coffee shops, parks, beaches, or other public places.

3.4. Non-Combatants

The yardwork guerrilla relies on the support of people in the zone. Most yardwork guerrillas have *a spouse* or *a partner* without whose unequivocal support (or at least tolerance) the success of guerrilla yardwork would hang in the balance. Spousal or partner support can take many forms:

"Without question, the fountainhead of guerrilla [yardwork] is in the masses of the people, who organize guerrilla units from themselves. A guerrilla group ought to operate on the principle that only volunteers are acceptable for service." -Mao Tse Tung, re-interpreted

- *Combat.* The spouse joins the yardwork guerrilla in the yard, taking up tools to help execute various projects.
- *Supply.* The spouse purchases provisions for the yard and the household.
- *Nourishment.* The spouse prepares meals and refreshments to keep the G.Y. well-fed and strong for combat.
- *Morale and comfort.* The spouse offers words of encouragement, shares physical intimacy, and generally fulfills other emotional needs.
- *Medical.* The spouse treats wounds, injuries, and aches suffered in battle.

Small children can support the guerrilla by remaining in safe areas. In ages when their first priority is play, they must keep their activity confined to approved areas away from the battle front to avoid harm and other side-effects of combat. As soon as they are receptive to yardvolutionary indoctrination and able to provide meaningful help, they must be engaged in combat support operations, such as fetching of beer or tools, or clearing debris. *Older children* can be successfully employed in combat operations.

Family members, friends, acquaintances, colleagues and co-workers, neighbors, passersby, representatives of service or product vendors, e.g. electric or gas company, landscape supply truck driver, delivery truck driver, as well as the offspring thereof, constitute the outside circles of population.

Neighbors, particularly those with properties bordering on the yardwork guerrilla's, play a special role. In the best-case scenario, immediate neighbors can support the G.Y. in various ways, creating an environment of opportunity and allowing to expand the combat area. In the worst-case scenario, immediate neighbors can sabotage the yardwork guerrilla's efforts by physical obstruction or destruction, or by disapproving, disagreeing, or dissing. Such negative atmosphere creates an environment of isolation, encirclement, and besiegement. In most cases, neighbors will fall somewhere between these extremes. The absolute minimum any neighbor can do is to practice the American attitude of minding his own business and letting the yardwork guerrilla do likewise. The withholding of negative, sarcastic, critical, or judgmental comments about the appearance of the insurgent's yard takes on a special importance considering the wild, never-finished state there. Good neighbors join combat operations by lending a hand in projects; loaning tools or machinery; sharing information or early warnings; expressing approval or admiring the results of G.Y.'s work; or offering or asking for advice.

Civil authorities are another special case. The yardwork guerrilla must avoid drawing attention from any municipal bureaus.

He must abide by all local rules and regulations. He must keep the sidewalk, road, median strip, and all other right-of-way areas clear of obstacles and clean of debris. He avoids agreeing to Trojan-horse offers such as discounts on the planting of trees on the street that come without leaf-removal service.

Family members and *friends* can support the yardwork guerrilla by helping in battle, by verbal encouragement, or by simple words of appreciation. *Passersby* tend to at least say hello, and many share positive comments on the yardwork guerrilla's work. Especially if they ask questions about particular features of the front yard, such as plants or decorative elements, the yardwork guerrilla can attempt to recruit them for the yard revolution.

3.5. The Enemy

The yardwork guerrilla distinguishes between Bad and Good Nature. Bad Nature, her opponent, comprises everything she wants to eliminate, purge, greatly reduce, or keep out. In short, Bad Nature comprises everything that clashes with the G.Y.'s vision for the yard.

By contrast, Good Nature comprises all elements the guerrilla yardworker wishes to establish, keep, or cultivate. Throughout her struggle the G.Y. co-opts Good Nature to her ends, taking advantage of the changing seasons, the sun and the rain, the day and the night, to plant and sow as she wishes. She learns about Nature in order to master Her. When, for example, she replaces a lawn with a row of potatoes, she replaces Bad with Good Nature, using Nature's own weapons for her own ends. The guerrilla knows she cannot annihilate the mightier foe, so she strives to integrate Nature's

"The way of nature is unchanging."
-Lao Tsu

cooperative, flexible, and beneficial elements into the order she envisions to establish.

Fighting Bad Nature and cultivating Good Nature requires that the yardwork guerrilla respect Nature overall (in fact, the person most likely to become a guerrilla yardworker is a Nature lover). Bad and Good Nature constitute opposite sides of the same coin, operating on the same principles and striving for the same thing: survival. When respect for Nature vanishes, the yardvolution has lost.

3.5.1. Knowledge of the Enemy

To gain a correct strategic view for battle, the guerrilla yardworker must fundamentally analyze his opponent's resources and modes of action. At every stage, the insurgency must assess the situation to determine the necessary course. Keeping in mind his final goal and strategic considerations, the guerrilla yardworker then selects the tactics best suited to achieving the desired outcome.

> "When men lack a sense of awe, there will be disaster."
> –Lao Tsu

Rather than to know every possible detail at all times, the guerrilla yardworker needs only a general awareness of the major factors affecting his struggle. He must know just enough. The yardwork guerrilla espouses learning by doing. Action is preferable to preparing for action; the guerrilla yardworker must not spend studying the time he can spend fighting.

Nature's basic operating principles as they pertain to the conflict over the yard are as follows:

- *Seasonal cycles.* Seasons result from the revolution of the Earth around the Sun and the tilt of the Earth's axis. Some form of seasonal progression occurs wherever yards exist. The characteristics of each season differ by climate zone. In moderate climates of the

Northern Hemisphere, where guerrilla yardwork has originated, for example, seasons proceed from spring to summer to fall to winter and circle back to spring where the cycle begins anew (while spring tends to be considered the beginning of the seasonal cycle and winter its end, by definition a cycle with

repeating phases has no beginning or end). Spring, summer, and fall are productive seasons for most plants, while winter is for rest.

- *Green side up.* Plants grow from their roots in the ground upward in the direction of the sun in the sky.
- *Water.* Dihydrogen monoxide constitutes basic necessary nourishment for all plants.

Even such basic knowledge allows the guerrilla yardworker to adapt his actions to Nature's. The long-term character of his cause dictates learning about Nature in gradual fashion. With each engagement, the G.Y. improves his knowledge of the adversary until he is familiar enough with Her for all his action to be strategically sound.

3.5.2. Enemy Agents

Nature possesses no conscience or consciousness, either of Herself or of the yardwork guerrilla—Nature just is. She continues Her relentless evolutionary march through time. She has been there since the beginning of time and will be there until its end. Nature grows plants that are best adapted to the environment and guarantee the greatest rate of survival. Without cultivation and maintenance, any plant can be overtaken by Nature's stronger, more vulgar agents. In the yard, Nature does only what its owner allows. To assert his will and turn his vision for the yard into reality, the yard owner must fight Bad Nature to restore Good Nature to Her rightful place.

Bad Nature's agents include:

- Diseases and fungi attacking desired plants
- Weeds, invasive plants, non-native plants, and all parts thereof, including roots, stems, leafs, flowers, fruits, and seeds, as well as all unwanted plants
- Insects that are harmful or annoying, and pests, such as aphids, some beetles, worms, or mites
- Mollusks, such as slugs and snails, and other non-mammal pests
- Some birds, especially pigeons and all fruit-stealing birds
- Mammal critters and varmints such as mice, rats, moles, gophers, or squirrels; neighborhood cats that mistake his yard for a toilet; and larger mammals such as coyotes, deer, and raccoons

Fighting each enemy agent requires different tactics of defense and counter-attack, including physical barriers, physical control (removal, traps), biological substances and concoctions, and Good Nature agents (beneficial insects, plants, birds, and animals that repel, kill, or feed on Bad Nature's agents). The yardwork guerrilla avoids using synthetic fungicides, herbicides, and pesticides. Rather than individual plants, he focuses care on the soil because healthy soil provides the best protection. (For detailed advice on fighting specific pests, consult the resources listed in Sources and Inspirations.)

"When the forces of oppression come to maintain themselves in power against established law, peace is considered already broken."
-Che Guevara

Features of the yard's terrain can be adversary too. If the yard's dirt is too rocky, Bad Nature includes rocks; if it's too sandy, sand. A creek cutting through the property and eroding its banks or flooding; a slope that's sliding down; or a tree stump rotting in the ground can all be Bad Nature.

Excessive encroachment of Bad Nature into the yard provides the stimulus for guerrilla yardwork. Each individual guerrilla yardworker will define excessive and bad in his own way: for some it will be a lawn, where planter beds should provide sustenance, for others it will be weeds and ivy spreading unbridled where a grove of pines should sway in the breeze. Overgrown blackberry bushes can occupy the area where a hedge should provide separation; a tree can prevent the full force of daylight from entering the dwelling; or a tree can stand in the path to the future patio.

"There is no greater catastrophe than underestimating the enemy.
By underestimating the enemy, I almost lose what I value."
-Lao Tsu

Where the potential G.Y. encounters a pristine, well-maintained yard, he can only fight to maintain it and keep Bad Nature at bay to prevent encroachment. Where peace and order prevail, warfare has no place; watering and trimming are peace-time activities.

While yardwork guerrillas fight many of the same elements in yards across the land, each has his own definition of Bad Nature and what constitutes it. One's weed is another's need; one's crop is another's crap. Dandelions can be sworn enemies or sources of tea-infusion leaves. Ornamental grasses can create visual harmony or inflict allergic reactions. A birch can lighten the atmosphere or remind of Russia. The beauty of guerrilla yardwork rests in the fact that the insurgent can define the enemy and cooperate with those elements of Nature that he finds beneficial. Hence the circle closes: to know the enemy is to know oneself.

4

Strategy

Guerrilla yardwork grows from a clear sense of revolutionary purpose. Its strategy utilizes the element of surprise to launch small, repetitive, and unpredictable attacks on Bad Nature's vulnerable spots at unpredictable times. The continuous blows weaken the adversary to the point of submission. Guerrilla yardwork relies on adaptability to changing circumstances; on flexibility, mobility and speed; and on local resources. In order to preserve his physical and mental integrity, the yardwork guerrilla only fights battles he can win.

> "Go forth without determining strategy and you will destroy yourself in battle."
> –Sun Tzu

4.1. Objective Conditions for Guerrilla Yardwork

Certain conditions must be met for the yardvolution to succeed. Subjective conditions relate to the agent of the yard revolution—the yardwork guerrilla. Objective conditions refer to various situational circumstances.

4.1.1. Yard Ownership

In theory, guerrilla yardwork can be conducted in any yard, but only in the yard that the yardwork guerrilla owns can she achieve true supremacy. Home and yard ownership is a necessary condition for the emergence of every yardwork guerrilla. Human nature focuses a property owner's energy on quality maintenance and improvement of the property better than renting or receiving payment for landscaping. Ownership triggers a unique desire to improve the owned property in order to increase both its enjoyment and market value. A yard attached to a rented dwelling, sublet, or apartment building may be *de facto* in guerrilla yardworker's charge for the duration of the lease, but it is ultimately under the property owner's control. Renters and proxy fighters, that is, men and women attempting to transform another person's yard, lack the financial and emotional investment of the home and yard owner. Guerrilla yardwork in a rental property faces the danger of subversion and counter-revolution at the property owner's whim.

Without exception, the dwelling is the primary object of the real estate purchase. The yard itself tends to enter into purchase considerations as a secondary factor. During the home search and purchase processes, the future guerrilla yardworker must seek a property with a yard that has the greatest yardvolutionary potential.

Ownership of the yard must be maintained. Monthly payments on a mortgage loan, the most common way to finance the real estate property that includes the yard, assure the continued possession of the yard. A solid, stable financial situation underpins the ability to make mortgage payments and depends on continued employment; salary increases through promotions or better jobs; business or investment success; a spouse with superior net worth or wage earnings; or a close relationship with elderly relatives. It is also advisable to remain married or linked in a civil union or other form of long-term relationship with the property's co-owner or co-habitant. A suitable physical and mental condition and a hard-drug free lifestyle are additional prerequisites (see 3.1. Guerrilla Yard-worker: Yard Reformer).

The yard the G.Y. aims to transform must be attached to her primary residence. Dwelling in the primary residence allows for intimate knowledge of the zone, including its ground, enemy, and surrounding areas and their population. Secondary residences, owned for vacation or investment purposes, cannot be used for guerrilla yardwork effectively because intervals between stays tend to be too long to facilitate guerrilla yardwork. Maintenance of land adjacent to investment homes is typically performed by renters or landscaping companies.

4.1.2. Enemy Presence and Activity
Guerrilla yardwork requires that Nature be present in the yard. Yards that are paved or covered with stepping stones, bricks, or gravel cannot accommodate guerrilla yardwork. In such cases, the dedicated guerrilla yardworker de-paves the yard and replaces artificial materials with Good Nature (see also 3.5.2. Enemy Agents).

4.2. The Strategy of Guerrilla Yardwork

Each guerrilla yardwork strategy relates to all others. Depending on the operational picture, emphasis rests on different elements at different times and locations around the yard. The strategies overlap significantly, so that one cannot be executed successfully without implementing one or more of others.

Apart from being a method of transforming the planet, guerrilla yardwork is both a state of mind and a way of life. Each strategy sprouts from philosophical roots (see 1. Purpose and Politics) and translates into a set of tactics (see 5. Tactics).

Both dynamics depend on the guerrilla's personal orientation toward self-reliance, concentration of attention to one's thoughts and actions, and focus of spirit toward the Earth. Individual yardwork guerrillas may have various aphorisms to live by, but they will all agree on the validity of three commonly known rules that underpin, pervade, and blanket the philosophy, strategy, and tactics of guerrilla yardwork:

- "Do it yourself."
- "Get by with what you have."
- "Leave no trace."

4.2.1. Accept Change as Constant

In keeping with the underlying drive to overturn the status quo, the yardwork guerrilla must initiate change and ensure it continues. Change in the yard alters the environment for the struggle, which, in turn, influences action to follow. A feedback loop forms.

> "Determining changes as appropriate, do not repeat former strategies to gain victory."
> –Li Quan

The character of guerrilla yardwork shifts constantly, so the yardvolutionary must adopt change as his way of life despite the social pressures springing from adulthood (see 1.1.4. Heed Others' Expectations). For the G.Y. stability equals stasis, predictability causes boredom, and comfort leads to laziness. He avoids the ossification of settling down; he eschews the calls for slowing down; he resists the onset of "I'm old" thinking. For the G.Y., change is the only constant.

4.2.2. Adapt to Circumstances

Given persistent change, the yardwork insurgent must adapt both to environmental changes she initiated and to those beyond her control, particularly the weather. Nature changes with the season as well as monthly, weekly, daily, and hourly. Nature's movements can be predictable and relentless, occurring with no master plan, strategy, or regard for human intentions. Everywhere, including the yard, Nature will do what She does whether the yard-volution proceeds or not. The need to adapt to circumstances, therefore, exerts a constant pressure on the G.Y. Such changes require that the guerrilla constantly modify her tactics and take advantage of each situation. Flexibility is key. In every locale and in every season, guerrilla yardwork makes for a fluid activity. Successful combat applies a different combination of tactics in different situations, as Bad Nature reacts to the insurgent's actions and the insurgent to Bad Nature's.

Circumstances change in other areas as well:

- *Urban living events.* Trash, recycling, and composting disposal schedule can influence the timing of some battles. Holidays such as Independence Day, can generate the need for extra cleanup or brush fire suppression; others, such as Thanksgiving, Christmas, or New Year's, force extended pauses between battles. Street work, such as sewer repair or power line maintenance, can also disrupt progress.

"[T]he ability to gain victory by changing and adapting according to the opponent is called genius."
-Sun Tzu

"[T]he guerrilla fighter must have a degree of adaptability that will permit him to identify himself with the environment in which he lives, to become a part of it, and to take advantage of it as his ally to the maximum possible extent. [A] fundamental characteristic of the guerrilla is his flexibility, his ability to adapt himself to all circumstances, and to convert to his service all of the accidents of the action. [T]he guerrilla fighter invents his own tactics at every minute of the fight and constantly surprises the enemy."
-Che Guevara

- *Municipal regulations.* In well-established incorporated or municipal locales, regulations pertaining to residential areas change little and infrequently. But when they do, they can affect the yard transformation, typically by adding to the list of tasks. The yardwork guerrilla pays close attention to and prepares for all changes in her city's regulations.
- *Neighbors.* Whether they are yardwork guerrillas or not, neighbors modify their yards, too. They plant or cut trees; they build or tear down structures; they feed or kill squirrels or birds. The yardwork guerrilla must anticipate and respond to all moves by her neighbors that affect her struggle.
- *Spouse.* Whims of a life partner are not to be taken lightly. Because they often take the form of a request, an imperative, or an ultimatum, they greatly affect the yard revolution's course. The yardwork guerrilla must be prepared to respond to demands for new plants, 'suggestions' for new projects, and unpredictable changes of mind. Having cultivated the ability to pick her battles, she goes with this flow.
- *Self.* As the yardvolution progresses, so does its agent. The G.Y.'s overall vision for the yard may evolve as she transforms the yard. At other times battle outcomes will fall short of the envisaged result, forcing corrective action (see 3.2.2. Revolutionary Consciousness and 3.2.3. Character of the Yardwork Guerrilla).

The yardwork guerrilla's ability to adapt to changing circumstances rests on knowledge of the enemy (Bad Nature) and on repeated situational assessments, both of which, in turn, depend on the guerrilla's attention, alertness, and acuity. The yardwork guerrilla must focus all her senses and intellectual capacity on observing the situation and make correct interpretations of facts. Every step depends on the previous one and influences the next one.

4.2.3. Strike First, Strike Often, Strike Fiercely

Inferiority in strength vis-à-vis Nature forces the yardwork guerrilla to his primary strategic posture—offense. Once he gets on the defensive, loss looms. Even actions that are defensive in their objectives can be performed in an offensive manner: by movement, dispersion, withdrawal, diversions, and counter-attack. Given Bad Nature's lack of inhibitions, the guerrilla yardworker must initiate engagement. Initiative helps him attain and retain a greater sense of control over the battlefield. The proactive approach allows the yardwork guerrilla to seize initiative and quickly shift to offense even if forced to retreat or withdraw. Seizing initiative propels him toward the revolutionary yard change he seeks. Strike by strike, he shovels ever closer to his ultimate vision.

Initiative brings manifold advantages to the guerrilla:

"After causing panic by surprise, he should launch himself into the fight implacably without permitting a single weakness in [himself] and taking advantage of every sign of weakness on the part of the enemy. Striking like a tornado, destroying all, giving no quarter unless the tactical circumstances call for it, judging those who must be judged, sowing panic among the enemy combatants..."
-Che Guevara

- *Time and place.* The side that strikes first chooses the time and location of engagement. With the selection, the insurgent determines two of the most important aspects of battle and sets its tone. The first strike allows for better preparation and planning.
- *Control.* The first strike also allows for greater flexibility in decision-making and action. If the insurgent decides

the Where and When of battle, he can decide its other aspects as well. The insurgent's initiative forces Bad Nature to react to attack and constantly scramble forces to retain territory.

- *Element of surprise.* Striking first aids the G.Y. in achieving the fundamental tenet of guerrilla yardwork: the element of surprise. The unexpected nature of attack provides crucial advantage in battle (see 5.2.1. Element of Surprise).
- *Randomness.* When the blows come repeatedly at unexpected times and locations around the yard, they begin to acquire a pattern of near-randomness, forcing the enemy to fight on many fronts at the same time.

Seizing and maintaining initiative highlights the importance of knowing the self and the enemy. An overly pessimistic estimate of the situation on the ground can force the revolutionary into a cautious, passive stance leading to loss of initiative. An overly optimistic situational assessment can result in premature action, burn out the yardwork guerrilla, and lead to the same result.

"Attack when they are unprepared, make your move when they do not expect it."

"In battle, confrontation is done directly, victory is gained by surprise. If you cause opponents to be unaware of the place and time of battle, you can always win."
–Sun Tzu

Another way to lose initiative is to vacate the theater of operation and abandon combat for a prolonged period of time, whose length will depend on the season or weather. On occasion, circumstances in the guerrilla yardworker's life, such as vacation, sickness, household chores, hobbies, or relationships, may prevent him from engaging in combat. In other instances, the guerrilla may execute a tactical retreat. During such periods of inaction, Bad Nature may regain initiative.

Regaining initiative after a period of retreat is much more difficult than remaining on the offensive following a victory. The yardwork guerrilla avoids being maneuvered into losing initiative and forced to attack.

Should the yardwork guerrilla lose initiative, he must first extricate himself from the passive position by delivering a blow or two in some area of the yard. Initially the blows can be random, such as mowing the lawn or cutting off a dead tree limb, but later they should conform to a plan or contribute to the progress of a project. Thus the G.Y. can wrestle some degree of initiative back from the adversary. Though exchanges of initiative may appear to conform to the undesirable two-steps-forward-one-step-back scenario, attempts to seize and retain initiative prevent the yardvolution from losing momentum. Greater tactical success results when striking unpredictably and swiftly, even if it means a temporary retreat.

Strikes repeated at various times and locations demonstrate the insurgent's resolve and weaken Bad Nature to the point of retreat, allowing the insurgent to establish supremacy. Persistence and endurance pay off as continuous blows alter the balance of power in the yard. Where Bad Nature goes on the defensive, the yardwork guerrilla can encourage Good Nature to step in and prevail.

To continuously strike, retain initiative, and assure the element of surprise, the yardwork guerrilla has a number of projects under way, so that he can carry out each battle separately, in a different area of the yard and at different times. At an opportune time he strikes, fights to win, then withdraws. Back at the base he prepares for another strike in an area that of-

> "[I]t is the side that holds the initiative that has liberty of action."
>
> "It is apparent that we can gain and retain the initiative only by a correct estimation of the situation and a proper arrangement of all factors."
> -Mao Tse-Tung

fers the greatest advantage. Pushing with maximum speed, he launches the strike. The strike-withdraw-strike cycle assures continuity of combat. It leaves Bad Nature with no time to recover between battles and forces Her to fight constantly and on many fronts.

Continuous blows also allow the yardwork guerrilla to carry the momentum. The completion of each project phase, successful strike, and victorious battle generate excitement for the next one. Seeing immediate results fuels passion for the fight and builds strength for the next battle. Conducting concurrent projects creates room for error without the discouragement brought by defeat: even if the yardwork guerrilla falls short of achieving a tactical objective in one area, success in other areas assures he retains overall forward momentum. Each success counts as a victory and each victory, no matter how small, propels the guerrilla toward his final vision.

"The blows should be continuous."
-Che Guevara

4.2.4. Preserve Yourself

The guerrilla yardworker only goes into battles he can win without suffering casualties. He only undertakes projects he can complete by himself, or, at most, with minimal support from others, and within a reasonable time span, such as an afternoon or a weekend. He breaks complex projects into phases, the completion of each of which should take no more than a day's work. For example, the construction of a fence can be split into at least five separate battles. In the first battle the yardwork guerrilla makes measurements and digs the holes for posts. Next he secures posts in their location. The third battle involves affixing the rails, the fourth nailing the pickets. He finishes the fence by attaching toppers onto the posts. Each of these phases can be further divided by fence section, or the whole project broken down into phases corresponding to each fence section.

The yardwork guerrilla only attacks small areas of the yard and finishes what he started there before proceeding to another area. In multi-phase projects, the entire project need not be completed before starting the next one. Rather, the yardwork guerrilla proceeds by phases: if a phase of the fence construction project is completed, for example, he can next work on a phase of a different project before resuming the next phase of the fence. By biting off only what he can chew, the yardvolutionary ensures that, morsel by morsel, he will eat the whole meal; by sampling different meals at different times, he will never go hungry or suffer from lack of variety. Practicing restraint in battle aids the yardwork guerrilla in achieving continued success.

The yardvolutionary must retain a self-preservation outlook. Prior to battle he must take measures in order to emerge unharmed and suffer no casualties, such as injuries, wounds, exhaustion, or loss of motivation. Safety precautions ensure not only that he retains his health but also that the revolutionary spirit survives. He wears well-fitting clothes, which he complements with protective equipment (see 5.1.5. Arm Yourself: Yardwork Guerrilla's Equipment). When forced to operate machinery, e.g. a weed whacker or rototiller, he first reads and then follows the instruction manual. During battle,

"The tactics of defense have no place in the realm of guerrilla warfare."

"Even in defense, all our efforts must be directed toward a resumption of the attack, for it is only by attack that we can extinguish our enemies and preserve ourselves."
-Mao Tse-Tung

"Those skilled in defense hide in the deepest depths of the earth, those skilled in attack maneuver in the highest heights of the sky. Therefore they can preserve themselves and achieve complete victory."
-Sun Tzu

he takes breaks to assess his progress, prepare for the next assault, or refresh himself with snacks and non-alcoholic fluids (interspersing glasses of water, juice, or lemonade with a domestic lager can calm and slow his body and mind, taking the edge off the stress of combat). Following victory he retreats to rest, gather strength, and fulfill his other chores. Between battles, he conditions his body to restore strength and build endurance through healthy nutrition and exercise; through intellectual, creative, or social activities he fortifies his mind, refreshes the consciousness of his revolutionary purpose, and enjoys the amenities of the Internet's virtual sanctuary (see 5.5. Activities In-Between Combat Operations).

The guerrilla yardworker also assures his self-preservation by adapting to circumstances and retaining initiative. Flexibility in light of the changes in the environment and a high degree of mobility between projects makes the yardwork guerrilla a difficult, moving target. Like a stalk of grass that bends in the wind to prevent breaking, the yardwork guerrilla flexes with every new situation to avoid dangers to his physical and mental integrity. Overextension reduces the effectiveness of each engagement and leads to a loss of momentum. If the guerrilla fights on too many fronts, he can get mired in any one or more of them and spend more time defending meager gains than making progress.

As soon as survival is assured, the guerrilla yardworker fights to gradually weaken the enemy.

4.2.5. Weaken the Enemy

Given that it is impossible to stop Nature's momentum, the guerrilla strives to weaken Her bad parts. By attacking, reducing, and eliminating Bad Nature from the yard and encouraging, cultivating, and nourishing Good Nature, the G.Y. can weaken Bad Nature's resolve to encroach and entrench Herself in the yard (see 3.5.2. Enemy Agents). Like Chinese water torture, the small but continuous blows combine to break the cycle of natural selection, which tends to favor Bad Nature, and to allow the yardwork guerrilla to impose her will in the yard.

The first attack and battle should take place in an area directly adjacent to the house. The yardwork guerrilla selects a small area to transform with a project, attacks it with a single blow or in a small number of successive phases, until she establishes control over that area by achieving the desired result. The first battle serves as a test of her skill, resolve, and tactical prowess. The subsequent victory feeds her enthusiasm for further action. Each subsequent battle takes place on the yardwork guerrilla's terms: she selects the timing and location to assure the element of surprise and increase the chances of victory (see 5.2.1. Element of Surprise). The choice depends on the order of project priority, current circumstances, and resources available for battle. For example, if the yard needs a new fence but the yardwork guerrilla only has enough lumber for a garden bed, and it is spring time, the latter project comes first. When pitching battle farther afield in the yard, the G.Y. must first secure approach and escape routes (see. 5.1.3. Determine Routes).

> "The changes of unorthodox surprise movements are like the ceaseless changes of the weather cycle."
> -Li Quan

The *patchwork approach* to yard revolution may appear random and chaotic—that is, in fact, its chief advantage. Striking in random areas in order of subjective priority forces Bad Nature to redirect Her forces in unpredictable patterns. Over time, the G.Y. connects the disparate areas under her control and strikes in adjacent patches of the yard. Soon she expands control over larger and larger area. Conducting concurrent projects in various areas of the yard opens simultaneous fronts both along the adversary's flank and deep in the yard's territory, opening multiple windows of opportunity for delivering repeated, continuous blows. The most significant drawback of the patchwork approach is the difficulty of fighting in areas completely surrounded by areas under enemy control. Striking at the heart may be effective, but the encirclement poses challenges for maintaining control. Attack in such target areas thus requires clear superiority in terms of circumstances (weather, season), troop numbers (collaborative attack with additional fighters), and time (opportunity for continuous attacks over a short span). The attack on the middle must be supplemented by attacks in other areas so as not to allow the adversary to concentrate Her forces.

"We must make war everywhere and cause dispersal of [the enemy's] forces and dissipation of his strength."
—Mao Tse-Tung

An alternative approach to weakening the enemy is more systematic but also more predictable. In the so-called *centrifugal-and-concentric approach* the yardwork guerrilla first transforms and secures all areas immediately adjacent to the house before proceeding further toward the yard boundary. Creating a buffer zone between the house and the battlefront assures good defense of the operations base. The radius of each battle depends on the size of the yard, the project, and the selected tactic. With each foray the fight enters deeper into enemy territory, striking repeatedly until assuming supremacy over the yard. As the yardwork guerrilla progresses in this centrifugal, ink-blot fashion, she draws concentric circles around the house, all the way to the yard boundary, and further out to the street, as needed. As with the patchwork approach, more than one area at a time may be undergoing transformation.

The direction away from the dwelling and toward the yard boundary ensures the forward direction of the attack. It also ensures battle always takes place on Bad Nature's flanks, which chips away at Her strength in systematic fashion at Her weakest points. The forward direction helps secure supply lines and escape routes over the already-conquered, rather than enemy, territory.

"Little victories come quickly, and spur you onwards. Success builds confidence."
-Richard Reynolds

After seizing control over an area, the yardwork guerrilla holds it with maintenance and emergency actions, performed as needed. Even though maintenance and emergency actions defend the gains made through transformational actions, tactically they take the form of attacks. Areas closest to the house take priority and the direction is, again, forward and outward, from the house to the yard boundary (see 5.2.2. Tactical Maneuvers).

In addition to her primary residence, the guerrilla yardworker may establish alternative bases, such as a shed or an accessory dwelling unit (colloquially, a 'granny unit'). If family dynamics do not allow for the main house to serve as the primary base, the alternative base may supplant the home as the guerrilla yardworker's starting point. Action that proceeds from such alternative bases should also follow the concentric and centrifugal pattern.

An exception to the outward direction of guerrilla yardwork may be an urgent need to take action farther away from the home. The guerrilla yardworker may need to build a fence around her property where none exists to delineate the territory for her struggle; she may have to trim plants encroaching on a neighbor's property to cultivate goodwill; or she may need to clear the right of way to meet the city's legal requirements. After victory in such battle, the yardwork guerrilla reverts to the original plan.

At other times, battling for area supremacy will lead the yardwork guerrilla to continue extending into an area whose location does not follow the concentric pattern. The G.Y. then rearranges her priorities according to circumstances while keeping in mind the strategic objective of weakening the enemy. For example, a landscaping project may extend from the house along the yard's perimeter; a path may stretch from the deck to the middle of the yard where a patio is planned; or a number of planter boxes need to be placed in different areas of the yard. The completion of project phases in succession takes precedence over the principle of concentric action, but phases of a non-concentric project should proceed in the direction away from the house.

"[Guerrilla strategy] must be adjusted to the enemy situation, the terrain, the existing lines of communication, the relative strengths, the weather, and the situation of the people. [T]he basic tactic of [guerrilla warfare] is constant activity and movement."
-Mao Tse-Tung

The guerrilla yardworker weakens Bad Nature by repeated strikes, tormenting her on all sides to the full extent of her capabilities, always on the offensive. At the same time, she must oscillate between attack and withdrawal. Action in a given territory must come as a surprise, be rapid and highly effective, and be followed by an immediate withdrawal. Weeding, pruning, cutting, mowing, digging, and re-planting are some of the helpful, one-time tactics that allow for the easiest attack-to-withdrawal transition. Depending on their timing and other factors, the incessant blows will, over time, soften the enemy's resolve to encroach

Fig. 4   "Those skilled in defense hide in the deepest depths of the
earth, those skilled in attack maneuver in the highest heights
of the sky."

on the territory that the guerrilla yardworker controls or wishes to control.

Like the strategy of self-preservation, the weakening of the enemy dictates that guerrilla yardwork be a series of small-scale engagements in smaller, manageable areas. This helps prevent over-extension, which compromises the self-preservation strategy and leads to unfinished, and thus un-won, battles.

The strategy of weakening the enemy puts to rest the frequent objection that guerrilla yardwork is chaotic. The strikes may be unpredictable and multiple projects may be underway, creating an impression of constant construction or even disrepair. But there is a method to the apparent madness: the strikes are systematic and continuous over a long period of time. At every moment they create the impression that Bad Nature is surrounded. In the face of the tireless guerrilla yardworker fighting for a just cause, the repeated attacks grind down Bad Nature's morale and soften Her resolve to resist and counterattack. The relentless pursuit of revolutionary yard change generates momentum with a single directional arrow: forward.

> "When guerrillas engage a stronger enemy, they withdraw when he advances; harass him when he stops; strike him when he is weary; pursue him when he withdraws. In guerrilla strategy, the enemy's vulnerable spots are his vital points, and there he must be harassed, attacked, dispersed, exhausted, and annihilated."
> -Mao Tse-Tung

4.2.6. Mobility

Total mobility around the yard and beyond enables quick adaptation to change. The yardwork guerrilla's body is constantly on the move. Like a juggler who only holds one ball at a time while the others are in the air, the G.Y. always conducts only one battle at a time while one or more others are underway in other areas of the yard. He moves from area to area, project to project, depending on where the greatest advantage lies, resupply is secured, and victory is assured.

Mobility aids in seizing and maintaining initiative. When a window of opportunity opens, the yardwork guerrilla strikes (the quicker the victory, the better). When opportunity eludes him, he shifts to another area where the chance of victory is greater.

The principle of mobility applies beyond the yard's boundary as well. As a multifaceted, broad struggle the yardvolution cannot be contained within a fence line or a property boundary.

> "[G]eneral agreement exists that the principal element of our strategy must be mobility. [T]he guerrilla must move with the fluidity of water and the ease of the blowing wind. Their tactics must deceive, tempt, and confuse the enemy."

> "Dispersion, concentration, constant change of position-it is in these ways that guerrillas employ their strength."
> —Mao Tse-Tung

4.2.7. The Long March
The guerrilla yardworker possesses a unique vision of what her yard should look like. Regardless of how large or small the differential between the current and envisaged state, the revolution will not take place overnight. The yard transformation not only requires a long period of time, it may, in fact, never be achieved in full. A number of limiting factors lengthen the yardvolution:

- *Time.* Employment, relationships, marriage, housework, hobbies, and other obligations limit the amount of time available for guerrilla yardwork. The G.Y. must carve out the time for the yard revolution wherever she can, distributing the load over many phases. The key is to celebrate every victory, no matter how small.
- *Money.* The mortgage loan and other financial burdens of home and yard ownership place a strain on the guerrilla's funds. Guerrilla yardwork lends itself well to a

limited budget (but where it saves on money, it takes its toll in time).

- *Energy.* Even if the yardwork guerrilla has time and money for battle, she must find the energy to do it. Her day job, finances, relationships, and other issues sap her energy, so that the prospect of yardwork can seem like another obstacle to overcome. The key here is to see the yardvolution as essential to well-being and prioritize guerrilla yardwork over other activities.
- *Nature.* Given enough time, Bad Nature can easily negate any progress: weeds will grow through the bark mulch; a woodpecker will bore a hole in the smooth white bark of the birch tree; the rose and lilac bushes will grow out of control. To get ahead, the yardwork guerrilla must attack continuously, with short periods of rest between battles to give Bad Nature no respite.

Though these constraints make for a protracted conflict, guerrilla yardwork provides a feasible response: it makes the best of the available time by allowing for strikes anywhere in the yard at any time. Significant progress requires stringing together a large number of small, short-term victories. Consequently, the yardwork guerrilla must turn the war's duration into a strategic advantage. Several ways have already been mentioned: dividing projects and tasks into phases; striking continuously; striving for self-preservation; and proceeding in a centrifugal-and-concentric fashion. Surrender is not an option.

> "A great victory is one that lasts long after the battle is over."
> –Richard Reynolds

4.2.8. The Networked Struggle

The number of yardwork guerrillas multiplies the effect of each guerrilla yardwork strategy (3.3. The Yardvolutionary

Army). Each insurgent strives to alter the appearance of his environment and the character of his community. As an army, G.Y.'s fight for urban transformation on large scale (see 1.3.8. Change the Urban Aesthetic). Yard after yard, neighborhood after neighborhood, city after city, state after state, these yard-volutionaries transform acres upon acres of urban land. All the small-scale yard revolutions add up to a significant force that alters the face of the Earth (see 2.1. The Yard Defined).

4.3. Stages of the Yard Revolution

Different sets of strategies and tactics suit different revolutionary stages. In general, every yardvolution takes the following eight broad steps toward ultimate victory.

1. *Pre-purchase assessment.* A smart yardvolutionary prepares for the war long before she acquires the yard. Having read the *Handbook* as part of her preparation for the real estate purchase, she assesses houses and yards with the view of the potential for guerrilla yardwork and a successful yardvolution.
2. *Vision formation.* With the celebratory sips of sparkling wine on the first day of home and yard ownership, the soon-to-be G.Y. steps into the yard for the first look as its master. She will see in the yard before her a space ripe for transformation into one that better fits her vision for her home. She begins to hatch plans for the transformation of the yard, which she may commit to paper as a sketch.
3. *Decision Day.* The fresh guerrilla yardworker makes the decision to take up tools in the service of the yardvolution's cause.

4. *Initial situational assessment.* The incipient yardwork guerrilla assesses the initial state of the yard and measures the magnitude of the struggle ahead against her vision. Acknowledging her relative weakness at the outset, she works primarily to acquaint herself with the terrain and its surroundings, study the enemy, gather necessary supplies, and otherwise prepare herself for the struggle (see 5.1. Prepare and Plan for Guerrilla Yardwork Operations).

5. *Strategic defensive.* Having had time and space to make advances during the home and yard sale process, Bad Nature will have gained initiative, forcing the G.Y. to react. At first, the yardwork guerrilla operates on the defensive in order to halt Nature's encroachment—the yardvolution begins as a resistance fight. But the G.Y. nibbles at the adversary using offensive tactics to defensive ends and positioning herself to wrest initiative into her corner.

6. *Yardvolution.* Limited counterattacks under the initial defensive operations will combine to create a starting line for offensive operations. Employing the strategies and tactics outlined herein, the yardwork guerrilla begins to gain an upper hand and to transform the yard. The offensive phase constitutes the core of the guerrilla yard war. First the G.Y. gains area superiority, i.e. limited, temporary control over a piece of her property where Nature can strike back easily. With sufficient repetition of offensive tactics the yardwork guerrilla shifts to achieving complete area supremacy. At any given time, various areas of the yard will be under different degrees of control by either side; transformational actions will tilt control toward the G.Y.

7. *Defending gains.* Once the radical transformation of the yard concludes, the yardwork guerrilla must maintain

the momentum of progress. Protecting her accomplishments from Bad Nature's reactionary forces will occupy the bulk of her time now. Because guerrilla yardwork is a pure attack method, it conforms to the old aphorism, "The best defense is offense" (see 5.2.2. Tactical Maneuvers).

8. *Updating vision.* The yardvolution's cycle begins anew when the first-time home and yard owner identifies further radical changes needed in her yard. Whether forced by natural causes, such as a fallen tree, or an evolution in her views, an occasional revision of the yard's appearance or functionality will occur. The G.Y. recognizes not only that her struggle is a long one but also that it has no end.

> "The enemy is much stronger than we are, and it is true that we can hinder, distract, disperse, and destroy him only we disperse our own forces. The total effect of many local successes will be to change the relative strengths of the opposing forces."
> —Mao Tse-Tung

> "[G]uerrilla warfare is not passive self-defense; it is defense with attack."
> —Che Guevara

4.4. The Relation of Guerrilla to Regular Yardwork

Guerrilla yardwork differs from regular yardwork. Foremost, it has a higher purpose (see 1. Purpose and Politics). Every yardwork guerrilla combines various motivations into his own 'revolutionary purpose mix.' The elements of the purpose mix and their relative weight therein may change over time, but the yardwork guerrilla always has the yardvolution in mind.

Guerrilla yardwork also differs from the regular kind by virtue of method. By adhering to the strategies and applying specific guerrilla yardwork tactics outlined in this *Handbook* to achieve transformational objectives, the yardvolutionary determines, manifests, and differentiates his way of yardwork from any other way. The guerrilla path may seem tougher than the alternatives. Its agent may many times wish he chose another direction. But the satisfaction from the conduct in time crushes all doubts as to its superiority.

> "Under heaven all can see beauty as beauty only because there is ugliness.
> All can know good as good only because there is evil."
> -Lao Tsu

The yardwork guerrilla fights alone and independently in his own yard. He relies on his own character, physical strength, and tools to do battle. Every once in a while he makes physical or virtual contact or gets together with fellow insurgents to refresh the revolutionary spirit, share news of victories, and exchange tips for battle. But after every event, he returns home. The geographic scope of guerrilla yardwork is limited to within and just outside the property's boundary (see 2.1. The Yard Defined).

A further challenge of guerrilla yardwork stems from its rules of engagement. Proponents of regular yardwork can apply some of the rules selectively; the yardwork guerrilla applies all of them all the time.

- *Perform all work yourself.* The G.Y. fights his own fight—he pays no proxies or mercenaries to do his bidding. He weighs exceptions with great care, including in supply (tool manufacture, material delivery) and dangerous or specialized tasks (tree trimming, stump removal, concrete pouring). Aside from draining his limited finances, paying others to conduct combat operations defeats the yardvolution's purpose.
- *Limit the use of machinery to a minimum.* Digging in the dirt creates a bond with the soil and can yield unex-

pected findings (one guerrilla yardworker reported discovering an intact 80-year-old tincture bottle and toy guns while digging up a lawn in his back yard). Because most machinery must be rented, in the final accounting the time and financial outlays associated with the rental offset the savings.

- *Use no chemical agents* to fertilize the soil, kill weeds, treat wood or other materials, or clean surfaces. The G.Y. fights Bad Nature on Her own terms.
- *Plant mostly plants native to the yard's climate zone.* The yardwork guerrilla plants no foreign, non-native, or harmful invasive plants, and takes great care planting beneficial invasive plants, such as spearmint or ivy.
- *Conserve your resources.* The G.Y. minimizes areas that require regular watering. He prefers perennials and plants, such as fruits, vegetables, and herbs, that yield the best value per plant, square foot, or compared to the store-bought equivalent. He also aims to plant for yields throughout the growing season or for multiple harvests.

Guerrilla yardwork extends beyond gardening. In addition to planting and caring for the flora, it includes constructing and maintaining recreational, utilitarian, and other functional areas of the yard and all other activities performed in the yard (see 2.4.7. Yard Elements).

Finally, guerrilla yardwork differs from so-called 'guerrilla gardening.' Defined by its advocates as "illicit cultivation of someone else's land," or "gardening on another person's land without permission," target areas of guerrilla gardening include vacant lots, railway land, public squares, median strips, abandoned yards, back alleys, and any other underutilized land. Guerrilla gardeners and guerrilla yardworkers fight for the same thing: the transformation of the planet for the better. But whereas guerrilla yardwork comprises more than gardening and is confined to the agent's personal property, guerrilla gardening limits itself to the cultivation of plants in mostly public areas. As a result, where the yardwork guerrilla performs his duty openly, in broad daylight, without fear of being seen or getting caught, the guerrilla gardener carries out his attacks in secrecy, usually under a cover of night. Further, while both the guerrilla gardener and guerrilla yardworker respect, admire, or even love Nature, their motivations and goals differ greatly. The guerrilla gardener seeks to make a statement and provoke broader change with his action: he seeks to reclaim and repurpose abandoned or neglected land for aesthetic or productive purposes. No matter how many plots he gardens, a huge number of untended ones remain. The guerrilla gardener is never finished in his quest. His endless ambition carries within it the seed of his doom. The guerrilla yardworker confines himself only to his own yard—he knows his limits. He seeks to reclaim only the part of the world that is his by title. His motivation and goals, vary as they may from individual to individual, are much more realistic and attainable, and they carry within them greater potential for satisfaction.

5

Tactics

Strategic considerations of guerrilla yardwork find ground-level expression in its battle tactics. Every combat operation ought to proceed along a number of distinct stages. Some of the stages may overlap, but none can be omitted.

Preparation occupies a significant portion of combat operations; battle itself is but one stage in the process. At every step, the yardwork guerrilla asks: "Will the planned sequence of actions result in victory under the circumstances?" If at any point she determines victory is doubtful, she withholds the attack and either waits for a better opportunity or moves to another area.

The yardwork guerrilla follows Carlos Marighella's sequence of combat stages below. First, in Stages 1 to 5, the G.Y. must devote energy to preparation and planning. The actual combat comes in Stage 6. After the conclusion of combat, Stages 7-8 comprise follow up. Stage 9 is a transitional stage that closes the loop back to Stage 1 to prepare for the next battle.

> "There is no [yard-work] guerrilla worthy of the name who ignores the revolutionary method of action and fails to practice it rigorously in the planning and execution of his activity."
> –Carlos Marighella, re-interpreted

1. Investigate information
2. Explore the terrain
3. Study routes
4. Map
5. Arm yourself
6. Execute
7. Clean up
8. Retreat
9. Rest

Every yard project, whether it entails demolition, construction, or maintenance can be broken down into these stages. Let us examine each stage in detail, using an example of building a simple back-yard brick patio for illustration. The patio has been selected as an example for its deeply transformational nature and a fair degree of complexity; it creates a new yard element in several project phases.

5.1. Prepare and Plan for Guerrilla Yardwork Operations

One way to begin the revolutionary yard war is to simply grab a tool and start digging (see 3.2.2. Revolutionary Consciousness). But this path to yardvolution resembles running a marathon without training. One cannot build a patio off the cuff, for example. Better to make basic preparations before launching the yardvolution and each project, and to build on that foundation between battles.

Preparation before the war means the yardwork guerrilla

- solidifies his vision for the yard while retaining flexibility for modifications;
- learns the basic lay of the yard land;

- outlines supply and procurement routes;
- acquires the initial equipment and supplies;
- begins to exercise and eat better;
- introduces himself to the population of the zone, particularly neighbors;
- informs his spouse, family, and close friends about his impending preoccupation; and
- arranges areas of rest and relaxation inside the house.

Preparation for each combat operation mimics these steps on a smaller scale. It comprises intelligence operations, reconnaissance, establishing routes, and arming. In the brick patio project, the G.Y. must envision the final product, gather information about the operation area, determine access routes and gather tools and supplies.

> "Careful planning is necessary if victory is to be won in guerrilla war, and those who fight without method do not understand the nature of guerrilla action."
> –Mao Tse-Tung

5.1.1. Investigate Information

Intensive intelligence effort undergirds every combat operation. The yardwork guerrilla first investigates information related to the intended project. First she reviews pertinent sections of this *Handbook* both for instruction and for motivation. Then she collects information to aid in completing the project. She peruses relevant websites, magazines, and books. For the brick patio, for example, she learns how to build it, including steps and timelines; what materials and tools she will need (descriptions, quantities, prices); and where to buy everything (locations, opening hours). She also needs to check the weather

> "No one can become a guerrilla without paying special attention to preparation."
> –Carlos Marighella

> "Proper planning prevents piss-poor performance."
> –unknown

forecast, the spouse's whereabouts during construction, and any engagements she must decline. She keeps the projected target area under surveillance up to the moment of attack.

5.1.2. Explore Battle Terrain

Equipped with basic intelligence, the yardwork guerrilla explores the terrain of the objective area (see 2.4.5. Yard Terrain). She notes the perimeter's topography (slope, undulations, soil type) and enemy presence (plants, tree roots, sun exposure), and examines the immediate surroundings of the projected combat zone to be affected by the project. She incorporates the information into what she already knows from earlier intelligence efforts to fill any gaps in her situational assessment. For the brick patio, she conducts a close inspection of the target area and its immediate vicinity, noting possible obstacles.

"The quick intelligence that constantly watches the ever-changing situation and is able to seize on the right moment for decisive action is found only in keen and thoughtful observers."
-Mao Tse-Tung

Throughout her investigation, the G.Y. keeps in mind the greatest advantage she has over Nature: thanks to human senses, consciousness, and information-processing capacity, Nature can be observed, investigated, reconnoitered, and explored easily, without the ability to reciprocate (low-level mammals such as squirrels can certainly observe and react, but do so instinctively and lack the ability to predict the yardvolutionary's actions).

5.1.3. Determine Routes

With information about the projected objective area in mind, the yardwork guerrilla studies and determines the supply, procurement, and access routes. In this stage, intelligence begins to transition into planning.

Supply and Procurement Routes

Because the insurgent cannot accomplish anything with just his bare hands, he must establish smooth supply lines.

A limited amount of supplies comes from the yard itself:

- *Soil* constitutes the yard's land area. At the outset, the yardwork guerrilla must contend with soil he inherits from the previous owner. If needed, he can work to improve it: in bulk by excavation and replacement, or incrementally through aeration, fertilization, fallowing, and planting.

- *Water* comes from the dwelling and the sky. When using municipal water for watering, the G.Y. should experiment with amounts needed; in no case should he wait until his plants wilt. While he can do little to directly affect precipitation in his climate zone, he should find ways to use only it for watering, including rainwater storage and distribution systems. Not only is rain free, it does not exhaust the drinking-water aquifers in the zone. To reduce the need for watering, mulching should be employed to cover the top soil layer with additional material; in addition to moisture retention, mulch keeps down weeds (see 2.4.5. Yard Terrain).

- *Sun* provides all the energy the yard needs. It is plentiful, particularly in the period between dawn and dusk and during the growing season; free; and practically

> "Supply procurement will be organized in the form of a chain of merchandise in such a way that the more common articles are procured in nearby places, and the things that are really scarce or impossible to procure locally, in larger centers. As the guerrilla struggle develops, it will be necessary to arrange supply from outside the limits or territory of the combat."
> —Che Guevara

inexhaustible. Killing weeds by depriving them of sunlight, e.g. with black plastic sheeting spread over the ground, is the cheapest method of sabotage.

- *Seeds and shoots* come from plants in the yard. The yardwork guerrilla first accepts the vegetation he finds in the yard upon purchase. Throughout the yard transformation, he plants, weeds, and harvests as needed.
- *Fruits, vegetables, and herbs*, too, result from the previous owner's or from the insurgent's own efforts. In his first growing season, the G.Y. simply harvests what the previous owner sowed and plants his own garden the following year. Each subsequent harvest results from guerrilla yardwork.

Because the yard can, at best, complement the yardwork guerrilla's needs, most of the supplies come from outside the property and must be purchased. For projects like the brick patio, in fact, almost all the supplies need to be sourced on the market.

"[I]t is necessary that the organized lines of supply function perfectly."
-Che Guevara

The guerrilla must determine sources for all needed items, optimal routes to accessing them, the cost of each item, and frequency of purchase. Supplies will likely be located in more than one place of business. Big-box home-improvement stores, which typically belong to large national corporate chains, can often provide most of what he needs. More specialized purveyors, such as grocery stores, nurseries, or clothing stores, offer greater assortment in their respective product categories.

Supply lines radiate from the guerrilla zone to areas where supplies are for sale. As backdrop for organizing supply and procurement routes, the G.Y. must be familiar with his neighborhood and city. Cities come with shorter, quicker, and smoother supply lines (see 2.3. Relationship to the City). The yardwork guerrilla prefers stores within walking or biking distance despite their potentially higher prices because procurement from them requires burning no fossil fuels and takes less time. In most

cases, however, materials must be secured by driving to distant areas, often on his town's outskirts. In addition, the fewer the trips, the better, and with careful planning, larger amounts of needed supplies can be secured in a single trip.

Some supplies, such as dirt, bark mulch, rocks, bricks, or trees, will require either renting a pickup truck, if the yardwork guerrilla does not own one, or delivery by a specialized supplier. In addition to delivery, the guerrilla may also need additional services, such as

- Tree trimming or stump removal
- Excavation, such as is required for oil tank decommissioning, septic tank installation or removal, or sewer repair
- Roof repair or replacement
- Debris hauling or trash collection

The final point in supply lines to the yard is storage on the property. Both open and covered areas can be used for storing supplies and materials. For the patio project, the driveway, side yard, or back yard can be used to store rock, sand, and bricks. The garage or shed work best for tools or weather-sensitive materials.

When setting up supply lines, the G.Y. also plans for the disposal of yard waste. The resourceful yardworker purchases or builds a bin to compost suitable organic waste, which he then uses as natural fertilizer. An appropriate commercial hauler takes care of excess or unsuitable green waste as well as garbage and recycling. Rules regarding content, costs, and frequency of disposal will differ from city to city; cities with the more progressive and environmentally conscious policies offer collection of all aforementioned types of waste.

Routes of Combat Zone Access

Having determined the supply and procurement routes, the yardwork guerrilla proceeds to plan access to and from the combat zone. He must keep several considerations in mind: original and target locations, routes between the two, and timing of transport and delivery. For combat zone access, original locations include storage and staging areas where caches are kept prior to and after use. The primary target location is the project area. A special kind of a location is the waste disposal area. In the brick patio project, sod and dirt must be removed and stored away from the area. A pile in the corner of the yard, out of sight behind a tool shed is ideal. Alternatively, the G.Y. can dump the sod in the composting bin; disperse the dirt in other areas of the yard; make a pile in the front yard and stick a 'FREE' sign in it; or haul the sod away.

Next the insurgent plans routes from the storage or staging locations to the projected target area: he determines the paths he will take to fetch tools and wheelbarrow in the rock, sand, and bricks. Similarly, he sketches the necessary routes out of the project area, e.g. to wheelbarrow out the sod and dirt, or to clean up after finishing for the day. Depending on the layout of the yard and locations of the tools and materials, this can be a single route or multiple routes—the more locations, the more routes must be drawn between them. Every tool or load of material should be brought in from the staging or storage areas in a correct order and immediately prior to use, and put away immediately afterward.

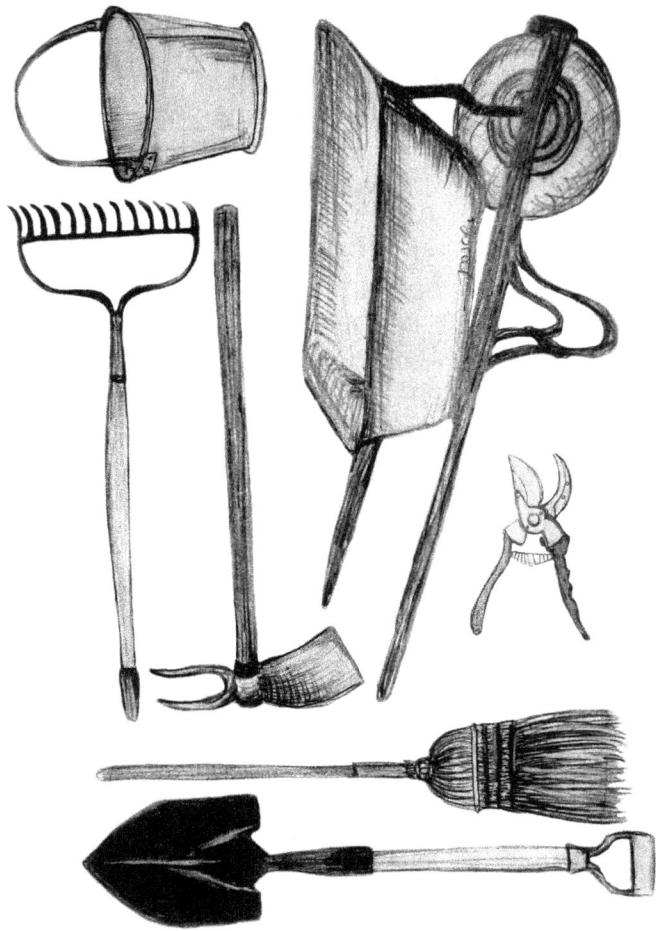

Fig. 5   "[G]uerrilla equipment will in the main depend on the efforts of the guerrillas themselves."

Such detailed route planning within his yard may seem excessive to many a yardwork guerrilla, especially if he has a smaller yard. The doubtful G.Y. should first consider the complexity of the project. Building the exemplary brick patio requires several phases—efficiency is of utmost importance. Often the most obvious route may not be the most efficient one. Multiple locations complicate matters further. To waste time walking circuitous or otherwise inefficient paths means to delay victory. What's more, space constraints in smaller yards place higher demands on creativity and planning. Finally, visualization helps move every project along, prepare for every step, and bring attention to previously overlooked issues.

5.1.4. Draw Maps

The yardwork insurgent superimposes her mental map of the area on her vision for the brick patio. A sketch hand-drawn on a sheet of scratch paper can help with the planning of more complex projects, such as the brick patio. Such a sketch may become a part of a larger map that outlines the ultimate vision for the yard.

Projects that alter the Earth's surface, e.g. the brick patio, which requires sod and dirt to be removed, benefit from marking the outlines of the projected target area on the ground itself. A round-point shovel (see the next section) can be used to make successive, overlapping cuts in the sod to delineate the shape of the future patio, with some extra room added as buffer.

5.1.5. Arm Yourself: Yardwork Guerrilla's Equipment

The G.Y. examines the tools and materials he already owns and purchases items missing from his arsenal, using the supply and procurement routes determined earlier. The equipment needed for guerrilla yardwork falls in the following categories:

- Tools (weapons)
- Plants and seeds
- Materials
- Food and liquids
- Clothing and footwear
- Medical supplies
- Miscellaneous accessory supplies

Within these equipment categories, equipment is either essential or accessory (secondary). *Essential equipment* must be acquired before the yardvolution and checked before each battle. *Accessory equipment* can be acquired in the course of the struggle as needed. In many cases, essential equipment can perform the functions of accessory equipment, albeit with lesser efficiency, e.g. raking leaves with a regular rake rather than a specialized leaf rake.

> "[G]uerrilla equipment will in the main depend on the efforts of the guerrillas themselves."
> —Mao Tse-Tung

Tools

Garden tools are the yardwork guerrilla's armaments. The choice of tools depends on need and finances. When it comes to tools, the yardwork guerrilla follows two general rules:

- Keep a limited amount of tools and instruments. A helpful guideline: "Only carry what you can carry."
- Use only tools that can be handled with the human body.

Light, non-mechanical tools are inexpensive to buy and replace. They allow for easy handling and transportation. They help maintain the connections between the insurgent's body and the Earth and between his efforts and their outcomes (see 1.3.3. Reclaim the Self). Easy to store, they require little maintenance and contribute little to nothing to environmental degradation during their use. Sourcing is easy: every neighborhood hardware store will have everything the G.Y. needs; tools at big-box stores will be cheaper, albeit at the expense of driving; yard, garage, and estate sales as well as second-hand stores may offer tools that are both cheap and tested in action.

Many yardwork guerrillas concede the advantages of an electric or gas-powered lawn mower, lawn edger, weed whacker, or rototiller. Steeped in the philosophy of guerrilla yardwork, the yardvolutionary acknowledges that his ultimate vision for the yard comes without a lawn (see 2.4.5. Yard Terrain). The area he wishes to rototill is too small for an efficient use of a machine. Greater satisfaction comes from manual transformation. Machinery comes with the hidden cost of maintenance and supplies, including oil, gasoline, and replacement parts to keep the equipment running smoothly (see 2.4.5. Yard Terrain.)

"[G]uerrillas are lightly armed attack groups, which require simple equipment [that] cannot be furnished immediately but must be acquired gradually."
–Mao Tse-Tung

The basic tool of guerrilla yardwork is the *round-point shovel*, so versatile a tool that it can perform the functions of most other garden tools. It is also the only tool needed to launch the revolutionary yard war. The uses of the shovel include digging holes for plants and construction projects; cutting sod, stems, or small roots; loosening the soil, aeration, and tilling; and transferring loose materials (dirt, bark mulch, debris) or dead animals (rodents, birds). In emergencies it can also be used to repel wildlife, such as squirrels or raccoons. The shovel is also an excellent prop for propaganda photographs. In the brick patio project, it helps dig out sod and dirt from the target area. The best blade material is tempered steel, which is not only strong, it can be sharpened if needed. Handles come in different lengths (39, 46, 48, or 57 inches) and materials, including wood (ash, hickory) and fiberglass. Fiberglass is stronger and more durable; wood is a renewable material and wood handles are easier to replace. Some shovel handles come with an end comfort grip.

Another essential tool is the *hoe*. The two-prong weeder hoe, also called combination hoe, offers greatest versatility. The flat, hoe end is used for piercing dried dirt and for chopping, weeding, or clearing vegetation. The pointed prong end is used for loosening the soil with precision, which aids in weeding closely around plants and for small weeds. Some insurgents prefer simple garden hoes but those offer much less precision than two-prong hoes, which are excellent for general garden cultivation. The hoe can help smooth the bottom of the hole for the brick patio or remove grass clots or plants from around the perimeter.

The *bow rake* helps loosen compacted soil, spread or level loosened soil and other material, and collect loose material onto a pile. In the brick patio project, it can be used to spread rock and sand on the bottom of the target area and collect debris after each project phase. Basic bow rakes typically come with 12, 14, or 16 steel tines (teeth), and 51- or 58-inch handles, though wider variants are available as well.

The *wheelbarrow* helps transport material, including rocks, sand, and bricks to the patio target area. The *bypass pruner* has two curved slicing blades and is used for cutting and trimming stems and branches, including those that may intrude into the patio area. The *plastic bucket* or *pail* is used for carrying, transporting, or storing smaller amounts of material, or for watering, particularly when planting. The *broom* is necessary for cleanup—a small push broom is the best, but a regular corn house broom is more versatile. It will come handy at the end of the patio project in spreading sand into the gaps between bricks. Some yardwork guerrillas also swear by the four-pronged spading fork, using one to cultivate soil and move bulky materials such as piles of weeds or compost.

The shovel, hoe, rake, wheelbarrow, bypass pruner, bucket, and broom are the essential tools of guerrilla yardwork. Every battle can be won with the help of these tools. Because each tool comes in a wide variety of makes, features, and specifications, the selection of a particular one depends on personal preference and budget. The G.Y. can test-run shovels borrowed from friends or fellow insurgents, or buy the cheapest tool to start and work his way to the kind that best fits his needs. In all, the essential guerrilla yardwork tools can be acquired for less than $100, though a higher-quality arsenal can total closer to $200. At the same time, following the aphorism, "I cannot afford to buy cheap things," the yardwork guerrilla selects only the best quality tools, designed for durability. Heavy-duty tools may come at a higher price, but they last longer and provide lower cost per instance of use and per their useful life.

"Oversharpen the blade, and the edge will soon blunt."
–Lao Tsu

In order to extend the useful life of tools, the G.Y. also devotes great care to their maintenance, keeping all his tools in good order. He only uses them for the intended purposes and in the intended way, avoiding excessive force and strain. After use, he cleans every tool thoroughly. When needed, he sharpens shovels and hoes with a metal file. After cracking or breakage, he replaces handles.

A number of accessory tools and instruments can increase the efficiency of guerrilla yardwork. The *square-point shovel* helps collect loose materials from hard, flat surfaces such as a sidewalk or a driveway. It can also be used to spread such materials, e.g. bark mulch, over the ground. The *leaf rake*, whose 24 or 30 flexible tines are arranged in a fan formation, is used for collecting leaves, thatch, and debris from the lawn and other areas with greater efficiency than a regular rake, whose tines are more rigid and prone to getting stuck in the grass. A *pick mattock* (pickaxe) is used for heavy-duty landscaping projects that require force the shovel cannot provide, e.g. trench excavation, hole digging, or breaking through tough surfaces. The *garden hose* with a watering front or rear trigger nozzle aids in watering. Gardening *hand tools*, including the trowel, the transplanter, the weeder, and the three-prong cultivator, offer greater precision for small garden projects or for use in pots or tubs. The large *wheeled container* or *bin* for organic waste provided by the city comes with home and yard ownership. The *composting bin assembly* can be used for discarding green waste and making natural fertilizer.

In addition to garden tools, the yardwork guerrilla should keep a tool box that includes

- 1 claw hammer
- 1 adjustable wrench
- 1 pair of tongue-and-groove pliers
- 1 tube of all-purpose adhesive
- 1 roll of duct tape
- 1 buck knife
- 1 hand saw
- 1 measuring tape
- 1 level
- 1 flat head (slotted) and 1 Phillips screwdriver
- 2 C-clamps
- 1 pair of protective goggles
- 1 metal file
- 1 toolbox
- 1 basic work table

These tools will aid in the repair of garden tools, construction of yard elements, and in various projects around the yard.

Devoted yardwork guerrillas swear by owning a *pickup truck*. More casual guerrilla yardworkers, owners of small yards, and owners of yards that require limited transformation may find the pickup truck unnecessary and instead fulfill their needs with their passenger automobile or with delivery services.

The brick patio requires a round-pointed shovel, a wheelbarrow, a measuring tape, stakes, string, a level, a rubber mallet, and a broom. A pickaxe can be helpful if the terrain is particularly difficult; a pencil and paper if a map is needed.

Plants and Seeds

In his vision for the yard, the G.Y. likely only sees rough outlines: a vegetable garden here, a shrubbery there, a shaded patio over there, and a rock garden right over there (a very motivated or ambitious yardwork guerrilla sketches his vision on paper). In choosing plants for his yard, he remembers that, as with any decision-making, too little information hampers decision-making and too much information stifles flexibility and can slow down progress. Even the most experienced or expert gardener finds the availability of hundreds, if not thousands, of plants challenging. Within his yard's topography and each yard element the G.Y. considers plants by the result he wants to achieve with them. For example, rather than mastering the characteristics of *Campanula* (bellflower) to fit it into the ornamental garden, he seeks a perennial with showy flowers.

To select a particular plant or a combination of plants for a yard element, the G.Y. considers his vision, the characteristics of his yard, and his budget. He seeks inspiration in area yards, in fellow yardwork guerrilla's recommendations, in plant labels at the point of sale, or in the advice of nursery staff. Many result-oriented categorizations of plants can serve as helpful guides, including the one below inspired by *Dirt Cheap Green Thumb*, *Guerrilla Gardening*, and *Sunset Western Garden Book*. Many plants fall into more than one category and many plants have variations that fall outside the primary category (each category features many more plants than the examples listed):

Color

- *Plants with showy flowers,* such as many perennials (chrysanthemum, foxglove, primrose); annuals (calendula, marigold, sunflower); bulbs (crocus, lily, tulip); cutting flowers (dahlia, daffodil, phlox); and landscape plants, including trees (acacia, dogwood, myrtle), shrubs (jasmine, lilac, sage), and vines (clematis, honeysuckle, rose).
- *Plants with colored foliage* (geranium, Japanese maple, lavender) *or fruits* (various types of berry, filbert, holly) provide color in a less dramatic fashion.
- *Fragrant plants* (butterfly bush, hyacinth, nasturtium) both smell good and tend to have showy flowers, too.

Landscaping

- *Trees of all sizes* (birch, hawthorn, linden)
- *Hedges and screens* (cypress, oleander, tea tree)
- *Vines* (grape, passion vine, wisteria)
- *Ground covers* (lily-of-the-valley, oregano, periwinkle)
- *Ferns* (athyrium, bracken, sword fern)
- *Ornamental grasses* (reed, ribbon grass, rush)
- *Palms* (coconut, date, palmetto)

Special Situations

- *Plants that attract butterflies* (columbine, manzanita, sumac) *and hummingbirds* (eucalyptus. fuchsia, gladiolus)
- *Plants for containers*, including pots, boxes, and baskets (crape myrtle, primrose, yew)
- *Plants for tropical effects* (banana, empress tree, poinsettia)
- *Plants to use near pools or ponds* (globeflower, juniper, yucca)
- *Plants for rock gardens* (echeveria, hebe, rockrose)
- *Plants for the sea coast* (tea tree, aloe, yarrow)

Problem Solvers

- *Plants for direct sun* (citrus, globe thistle, iris), *partial shade* (cyclamen, ginger lily, rhododendron), *or full shade* (hosta, lungwort, Solomon's seal)
- *Wind-resistant plants* (bougainvillea, daylily, pine)
- *Drought-tolerant plants* (agave, olive, rosemary)
- *Pest-resistant plants* (boxwood, lupine, magnolia).
- *Insect-repellent plants* (citronella, fennel, marigold). Any plant with yellow or orange flowers helps repel insects. As an alternative, plants that attract birds and beneficial insects can be substituted so that they fight amongst themselves and save the yardwork guerrilla a considerable amount of effort.
- *Beneficial insect-attracting plants* (cilantro or coriander, dill, mustard)
- *Poor soil-tolerant plants* (cactus, hazelnut, verbena)
- *Pollution-tolerant plants* (birch, hydrangea, sedum)
- *Weed-suppressing plants* (bergenia, cowpea, mazus)
- *Bird-attracting trees* (arborvitae, hemlock, spruce) *and shrubs* (barberry, black haw, elderberry)
- *Edible flowers* (borage, nasturtium, violet)
- *Fast-growing plants* (acacia, filbert/hazelnut, hibiscus)
- *Long-living plants* (forsythia, grape, rhubarb)
- *Healing plants* (aloe vera, poppy, spearmint)
- *Cold-resistant plants* (cabbage, echinacea, pear)
- *Productive plants*, including fruits (apple, apricot, cherry), vegetables (carrot, cucumber, tomato) and herbs (basil, chives, thyme)

This classification enables the guerrilla yardworker to make quick and reasonably informed decisions about what to plant and what to avoid. Because plants fall victim to Nature's whims, the guerrilla selects those that last longest and require the least maintenance: trees, shrubs, vines, and perennials best match this profile (the vegetable garden requires annual planting). Rather than obsessing about what he plants, the guerrilla focuses on the principle of how it's planted and cultivated. The adventurous insurgent plants whatever he wants wherever he wants, paying attention only to the tree/shrub/vine/perennial and sun/partial-shade/full-shade characteristics. Later he moves and removes plants as they come into their own. Experimentation requires patience: given that the yardvolution will last a while, the G.Y. manages his expectations regarding the results of his labor. Every plant takes a few growing seasons to fully establish itself, flower, and expand to its ideal size and shape. The yardwork guerrilla prefers plants native to his climate zone because they provide the yard with a sense of place, create a connection to the geographic region and its landscape, and attract native wildlife, including insects and birds. Naturally suitable to the local climate, native plants also require minimal care after they mature.

Every brick patio benefits from being surrounded by plants. The yardwork guerrilla selects a range of plants to complement the construction: flowering perennials to delight in the front areas; shrubs and trees for the back to provide shade.

Materials and Other Stuff

The yardwork guerrilla's principal material is dirt, which comes in various types and qualities. Most of the time, the dirt already present in the yard will do in the yardvolution. On occasion, however, it requires additions to enrich its composition. The main addition to the yard's soil is compost, a natural fertilizer resulting from the conversion of various organic materials. The resourceful G.Y. can make compost in a freestanding pile or in a purchased manufactured composter, such as a wire cylinder, tumbler, static bin, or, if he has room, a three-bin system. Ingredients of compost can include brown matter, such as dry leaves, hay, sawdust, straw, wood chips, and wood prunings, and green matter, which includes grass clippings, fruit/vegetable scraps, coffee grounds, egg shells, and manure. Layering the materials, sprinkling them with water, and turning them weekly for aeration helps all materials decompose in a manner of months. Other soil additives include peat and various organic fertilizers, such as fish emulsion, animal manures, blood or bone meals, sawdust, and meals made of soil-improving plants such as alfalfa or cottonseed.

The brick patio project requires small rocks or gravel, coarse sand, and bricks, all of which may need to be delivered by an outside supplier. Dirt and bark mulch can be used to fill the gap between the finished patio and the rest of the yard.

Food and Liquids

The yardwork guerrilla pays close attention to what he puts in his body; he is what he eats and drinks. His diet directly affects his physical and emotional states, which, in turn, impact his energy and motivation. Eating before battle provides the G.Y. with an energy input necessary for victory, while eating afterward helps restore his strength. He must also have a glass of water on hand for proper hydration (see 5.5.1. Cultivation of Health).

Clothing and Footwear

Guerrilla yardwork is not a fashion show. The yardvolutionary prefers well-worn *garments*, preferably those relegated from his primary wardrobe because they have already proven themselves in use, are more comfortable, and enable a greater range of motion. Being near the end of their useful life, used clothes can be soiled, abused to their material limits, and discarded more easily and with less regret. Quick-drying garments are preferable, as are dark-color fabrics. Outdoor or sports stores offer specialized selections of outerwear that will end up being used for guerrilla yardwork. Home-improvement stores or neighborhood hardware stores are best for items like gloves.

The yardwork guerrilla's *shoes* must be sturdy, with a thick treaded sole (Vibram is excellent), ankle support, and toe protection. Particularly in rainier climate zones, like the Pacific Northwest, the shoes should also be waterproof. At the same time, shoes should be as light as possible in order to prevent fatigue. Ideally, the G.Y. owns a reserve pair of shoes, such as old sneakers or hiking boots, for occasions when the primary pair is disabled, e.g. due to wetness. *Socks* provide a crucial complement to quality footwear. Thick socks, such as those used for sports or hiking, cushion the feet, protect them from impact, and prevent blisters. Two pairs of thinner socks can be substituted.

> "The vital necessities of the guerril-las are to maintain their arms in good condition, to capture ammunition, and, above everything else, to have adequate shoes."
> –Che Guevara

> "Uniforms are unnecessary."
> –Mao Tse Tung

The yardwork guerrilla's outfit is simple and functional. Light, long, and loose pants protect legs from exposure to the elements. Old hiking *pants* are particularly suitable because of their waterproof, quick-drying material and numerous pockets. A *T-shirt* is the base layer for the torso. Any material will do: cotton in particular is abundant in every wardrobe, but polyester wicks perspiration much better and dries more quickly. A light, *long-sleeve shirt* is helpful for chillier days or to protect from sun exposure. Men's polyester-cotton blend dress shirts offer both the needed functionality and the amusement of imagining the yard as the office. A thicker garment, such as a sweatshirt, helps on colder days. A rain jacket should also be kept on hand. A *wide-brimmed hat* protects the head and neck from sun exposure and bird excrement. Like shoes, *gloves* require special attention. A good pair of gloves protects hands from soiling and injury. Having two pairs of gloves on hand is recommended:

- *Fitted work gloves with a latex-coated grip* are ideal for projects where precision is needed, such as pulling small weeds, construction, or harvest.
- *Large leather-palm gloves* are best for heavy-duty projects requiring greater protection, such as digging, shoveling, tilling, or lawn-mowing.

Medical Supplies

No yardvolution can take place without some harm coming to the insurgent. Medical supplies must, therefore, belong to his arsenal. Medical supplies can be divided into preventative and remedial. Of the *preventative medical supplies*, high-factor sunscreen lotion or oil takes top priority. The insurgent must wear sunscreen at all times, applying it prior to battle directly onto the portions of his skin that will be exposed to the Sun and then every two or three hours thereafter, or as recommended by the lotion's manufacturer. Soap comes a close second; a bar of soap with solid particles, such as oats, is best because it provides gentle scrubbing action as well.

The first-aid kit contains in the minimum the following *remedial items*:

- Assorted adhesive bandages
- Compression bandage for bigger wounds
- Pain relievers, such as ibuprofen or paracetamol
- Medicinal alcohol for cleaning and disinfecting punctures, cuts, and other wounds
- A flask of vodka or other preferred spirit for dulling the pain of injury and comforting the soul
- Antibiotic cream for treating cuts and preventing infection

Complementary medical supplies include tweezers, scissors, and nail clippers.

Miscellaneous Supplies
Additional articles may not be absolutely necessary for the yardvolution, but they ease the challenges of the struggle. These miscellaneous supplies include three major categories of items:

- Accessory items
- Reused items
- Animal-repelling items

Accessory items include:

- 1 bottle, canteen, or other dedicated container to hold water during battle; can be substituted by a glass
- 1 plate, 1 fork, and 1 spoon (a durable spork may be substituted)
- 1 can of aerosol lubricant with an application straw
- 1 one-gallon canister of gasoline (full) or 1 electric extension cord with an accessible outlet for the lawn mower, if any
- 1 tire pump, if the wheelbarrow has pump tires
- 1 book or several magazines for killing time and for education during breaks
- 1 digital camera for documenting battles and record ing the revolution's progress (before and after photos are essential for propaganda)
- 1 notebook and 1 pencil or pen for documenting the struggle in narrative detail

Reused items are all manner of products past their useful life that can be repurposed as plant containers, barriers and dividers, construction materials, or decorative elements. Pots and teapots, pans, vases, crocks, tubs and bathtubs, toilets bowls, toys, shoes, crates, baskets, wheelbarrows, barrels, doll heads—any vessel that can hold dirt without decomposing can be used as a plant container (a hole must be drilled in the bottom of the container for drainage). Driftwood, large animal bones and antlers, and rocks can be put to decorative uses. Windows, doors and their respective frames, ladders, posts, planks, or trellises can be used for frames, dividers, and plant support. Almost any object can be put to use in the yard.

Finally, many objects can be used to repel the pesky agents of Bad Nature—animals. Human hair trimmings collected in a stocking and hung on a tree or bush branch help mark the territory as human and repel deer and rabbits. Any mirrors, sparkling garlands, or other shiny objects moving in the wind will repel deer or birds. Wire mesh wrapped around tree-trunks or made into barriers around seedlings will protect plants from being eaten. Urine poured from a collection vessel or, more feasibly, delivered fresh human-to-ground marks the territory. Various ingredients such as beer, rotten eggs, tobacco, or vinegar can be used against specific insects or animals.

"Within the framework of the combatant life, the most interesting event, the one that carries all to a convulsion of joy and puts new vigor in everybody's steps, is the battle. Combat is the most important drama in the guerrilla's life."
—Che Guevara

5.2. Execute the Combat Operation

Guerrilla yardwork constitutes a coherent and comprehensive philosophical, political, strategic, and logistical system. Yard combat follows a set of rules, within which the insurgent operates with great flexibility and speed.

5.2.1. Element of Surprise

Without exception the guerrilla yard-worker carries out her attacks in a surprise fashion; without the element of surprise guerrilla yardwork loses its essence. The absence of prior warning or indication as to the time, location, and manner of attack assures surprise. The hour of the day, the day of the week, the week of the month, the month of the year, and the season must be unpredictable or even seemingly senseless. The G.Y. attacks in any area of her yard she deems vulnerable or where an offensive is necessary. She avoids attacking in any chronological or geographical pattern other than when the time is right and the location fits the strategic outlook. On occasion, she may even attack when or where she feels like.

> "The basis of successful guerrilla combat is offensive action combined with surprise."
> —U.S. Department of the Army

> "Wage war with surprise moves."
> —Lao Tsu

> "The numerical inferiority of the guerrilla makes it necessary that attacks always be carried out by surprise; this great advantage is what permits the guerrilla fighter to inflict losses on the enemy without suffering losses."
> —Che Guevara

Timing

The element of surprise hinges on timing. The guerrilla yardworker strikes to seize and maintain initiative (see. 4.2.3. Strike First, Strike Often, Strike Fiercely), attacking in the time that is right for her and wrong for Bad Nature. Because this cannot always be achieved, the G.Y. determines the time of battle based on other considerations, especially convenience. Life obligations, including work, relationships, or hobbies, shrink the time available for the yardvolutionary struggle. Among the many things she has on her mind, plate, and agenda, yard time comes in limited supply. She must, therefore, squeeze yardwork wherever possible into her schedule. Following the principle, "It gets done when it gets done," the G.Y. draws up a list of tasks sorted by priority in terms of importance and urgency (the list can be unordered if the tasks are neither important nor urgent). As she executes and completes the tasks on the list, the G.Y. checks off each task. When the list becomes a jumble of checkmarks and notes, the G.Y. drafts another list, omitting the completed tasks, editing the tasks in progress, and adding new tasks. Alternatively, she updates the list on a regular basis, e.g. weekly, or when priority ranking of a list item changes. When yardwork takes place based on a subjective order of tasks, the time and form of attack remain secret. Additional benefits of the checklist method are thoroughness, efficiency, and portability.

Withholding attack when it's most expected can also come as a surprise. When everyone expects the G.Y. to launch an attack, as when weeds are several inches tall and beg for removal, *not* weeding can be unexpected. When the attack eventually does take place, the perceived delay or wrongness of its timing makes it all the more surprising. With delay each engagement gains in importance and intensity. The checklist method can be helpful here a well, though it ought not be viewed as a way to postpone battle out of convenience or laziness. Delaying attack for too long can make for a more difficult battle than necessary.

The growing season and the weather help select the time of attack. At first glance, winter may offer the greatest opportunity to attain the element of surprise, as no yard activity is anticipated, but low temperatures, snow cover, short daylight, and frozen ground present sufficient obstacles for the G.Y. to table the yardvolution for a few months to regroup, rest, and redraw plans. Though the spring-summer-fall sequence provides the basic yardstick, each plant should be considered individually (see 2.2. Climate Zone). As for weather, while the G.Y. can strike at any time, a cloudy and warm day is best suited for battle as it shades her from the sun, offers a pleasant outdoor temperature, and presents excellent visibility with just the right contrast. Too sunny and too hot, the yard becomes an oven; too much rain, a bath.

> "Those who know when to fight and when not to fight are victorious."
> –Sun Tzu

Some days are better for guerrilla yardwork than others. The industrious insurgent devotes weekends and so-called staycations to the yardvolution; an occasional mental health or fake sick day can also come handy. If working from home, days available for the yardvolution expand to the entire week: proximity to the yard saves time and yardwork itself becomes an active, useful respite from the travails of wage labor or contract work. However, the G.Y. must take care to balance the money-making obligations of work with the pleasure- and produce-yielding activities in the yard.

Sunrise and sunset bookend the ideal interval for yardvolutionary activity. Some evenings can be spent on small maintenance projects, like weeding or watering. Night work is not recommended. Visibility aids in the yardvolutionary struggle. To admire her labor's results, to fetch additional tools, or to take a nap under a tree in-between skirmishes, the G.Y. needs daylight. In urban residential areas, the only 'natural' lighting available at nighttime comes from street lights or surrounding houses. Floodlights mounted on the house exterior wall, work lamps purchased specifically for the purpose, or living room lamps brought out with extension cords can provide sufficient additional lighting for any guerrilla yardwork project, but daylight offers balanced light conducive to accurate situational assessment and precision in combat, particularly in complex projects like the brick patio. Artificial night illumination can also anger the neighbors. Noise poses an even greater obstacle to guerrilla yardwork in nighttime. Unlike during the day, when noise emitted in the yard merges with the din of traffic, child play, or music, night amplifies all isolated sounds. Keeping decibel levels down during nighttime maintains peace with the neighbors and prevents attracting unnecessary attention. The yardwork guerrilla uses night time to rest and recoup strength for her next strike. In sum, guerrilla yardwork ought to be conducted between winters and in daytime.

Target Selection

After selecting the time of attack, the G.Y. must choose her target. She has greater flexibility in target than in time selection. The patchwork or centrifugal-and-concentric approaches can both be employed with success (see 4.2.5. Weaken the Enemy). The skillful G.Y. can undertake any of the several projects in different phases of completion. To select the right one she proceeds in the order of priority based on importance and urgency. The project's intended outcome determines the importance; time, especially weather, determines urgency. The emphasis should always be on importance, not urgency.

Targets for guerrilla yardwork projects must be assessed along the following dimensions:

- *Criticality.* The destruction or major alteration of a critical target influences Bad Nature's ability to operate. Cutting tree roots, building a garden bed, or mulching fall into this category. Target criticality changes with the circumstances like the stage of the growing season or spouse's express wishes.

"In guerrilla strategy, the enemy's rear, flanks, and other vulnerable spots are his vital points."
–Mao Tse-Tung

- *Vulnerability.* The target's character determines its susceptibility to attack. The vegetable garden is best watered in the morning, the lawn is best mowed in the early evening. Target vulnerability also changes with the means available to the yardwork guerrilla. A leaking hose makes vegetables safe; a broken shovel protects the lawn.
- *Accessibility.* The ability of both the G.Y. and Bad Nature to infiltrate the target area affects its accessibility. Open ground is the most accessible, the corners and areas right outside the fence the least accessible. Areas closer to the house are more accessible than areas closer to the yard boundary. Accessibility shifts with seasons: spring increases accessibility, winter decreases it.
- *Recuperability.* Bad Nature's ability to restore a damaged target to normal operating capacity prompts recurrent attacks, such as maintenance. A lawn is a highly recuperable target—another reason to avoid having one. A weeded and bark-mulched area offers moderate recuperability, requiring occasional weeding and resurfacing every spring. A brick patio pushes recuperability close to zero.

The yardwork guerrilla keeps an assortment of targets on hand at all times (see 4.2.3. Strike First, Strike Often, Strike Fiercely). Not only does the yard naturally offer multiple projects and tasks to tackle, wide target selection allows for accommodating the guerrilla's personal disposition (energy level, thirst and hunger, mood), weather, and other circumstances (season, time of day, available length of time, checklist priority). It also facilitates the element of surprise: the enemy never knows which target will be hit.

The yardwork guerrilla concentrates her attacks on the enemy's flank—areas adjacent to those already under her control. The *head-on attack* entails tackling a task directly and without hesitation, e.g. pulling weeds, cleaning gutters, and trimming shrubs (in the case of plants, cutting off roots, vital branches, or useful parts such as leafs, flowers, or fruits, effectively disrupts their supply lines). Head-on attacks permanently or temporarily eliminate the enemy's vanguards, creating new vanguards that can be destroyed or damaged with later direct attacks. By contrast, *encirclement* entails working from the perimeter of the attack area toward the center. The brick patio project presents a suitable example: proceeding from the delineated boundary of the future patio, the G.Y. digs the hole for it from outside in, eliminating the enemy's forces in order to construct the recreational element (laying bricks from inside out is an operational maneuver, not a negation of the encirclement tactic).

"[T]he guerrilla does not consistently operate in one area but varies his operations so that no pattern is evident. If possible, he strikes two to three targets simultaneously to divide the enemy pursuit and reinforcement effort."
—U.S. Department of the Army

5.2.2. Tactical Maneuvers

Three kinds of yardvolutionary actions help challenge the status quo in the yard:

- *Transformational actions* modify the appearance and functionality of the yard. Offensive in character, they are essential to realizing the yardvolutionary's vision, and, therefore, take priority over all other actions. A 'before' and 'after' can be distinguished: transformational actions improve the state of the yard. Each completed project results from a series of transformational actions, which, in turn, lend themselves to organization into phases (see 4.2.4. Preserve Yourself). The brick patio construction exemplifies such a project. Following the completion of all preparation stages, the G.Y. first digs a flat-bottomed hole in the shape

> "[The guerrillas']
> tactics must deceive,
> tempt, and confuse
> the enemy."
> -Mao Tse-Tung

of the patio, accounting in depth for the thickness of all the layers and the altitude of the surrounding area. He spreads a layer of small rocks at the bottom, followed by a layer of coarse sand. After making measurements, the G.Y. then pounds the bricks into the sand using a rubber mallet, ensuring all the bricks are level. Finally, he uses a broom to spread sand into the gaps between the bricks. Each phase can be executed in sub-phases.

- *Maintenance actions* hold, preserve, and defend gains made through transformational actions. They tend to be easier than transformational actions and guarantee faster victory. Maintenance actions include mowing, watering, fertilizing, or weeding, as well as any seasonal actions such as trimming, seeding, or harvesting.

- *Emergency actions* prevent damage to the dwelling, yard elements, or the yardwork guerrilla himself. Emergency actions include removing a dead tree limb or an entire tree; preventing, managing, fighting, or controlling an onslaught or invasion of detrimental insects, invasive plants, weeds, and other pests; and repairing the damage caused by various varmints, vandals, or vagrants.

The three types of action translate into the following activities:

- Planting, sowing, seeding, potting and re-potting
- Trimming, cutting, pruning (thinning, heading, shearing, pinching)
- Weeding
- Deadheading (removing dead flowers and seed pods)
- Disposing
- Preventing, managing, and removing insects, pests, and diseases
- Fertilizing, feeding
- Composting
- Mulching
- Conditioning, winterizing
- Watering, drying
- Shoveling
- Digging
- Hoeing
- Raking
- Tilling, rototilling
- Soil solarizing
- Building, constructing
- Cleaning
- Storing

Each activity can be used in various offensive maneuvers, including the raid, ambush, and interdiction, variations of which are assault, penetration, occupation, execution, sabotage, and minuet. Psychological operations and intelligence activities complement these offensive actions. Each engagement includes contingencies for evasion and escape. The G.Y. maintains mobility through alert shifting.

Raid

A surprise attack against an enemy force or installation, the raid entails secret movement to the target area, brief and violent combat, rapid disengagement, and swift, deceptive withdrawal. Raids can be employed to various ends: to damage or destroy enemy agents or supplies (trim trees or shrubs); to capture supplies or equipment (harvest produce, i.e. pick fruits or vegetables); to expropriate enemy property, supplies, or equipment (cut flowers); to divert attention from other operations; or to keep the enemy off balance. Any task that can be completed with minimal preparation and with great speed qualifies as a raid.

Ambush

The element of surprise finds another natural expression in the ambush—a surprise attack against moving or temporarily halted targets. The ambush harasses or demoralizes Bad Nature; damages or destroys Her agents; delays, blocks, or diverts Her movements; or cuts off Her supplies. To weaken Bad Nature in the yard the G.Y. strings together a series of ambushes, attacking and withdrawing repeatedly in a hit-and-run fashion. In the ambush, Nature has a greater say in setting the time of the attack: the stage of the growing season or plant growth, the time of day, or the weather can encourage or hamper a strike. The G.Y. has greater control over the location of the attack. Examples of the ambush in the yard include weeding a larger area, raking leaves, lopping suckers, or selective watering.

> "Hit and run, wait, lie in ambush, again hit and run, and thus repeatedly, without giving any rest to the enemy."
> –Che Guevara

Interdiction

A cumulative effect of numerous smaller offensive operations, such as raids and ambushes, interdiction interferes with the enemy's movement and denies Her use of certain areas. Interdiction serves to establish control over areas and to regulate what grows there.

Assault

Assault is an armed attack to push back Bad Nature. It typically involves the destruction of Her agents or installations. Examples include brush clearing and large-scale weeding.

Penetration

A deep foray into Bad Nature-controlled territory constitutes a penetration. A penetration can gather intelligence, establish an outpost, selectively remove a plant, or recover a fruit.

Occupation

When the yardwork guerrilla takes over a portion of the yard, stationing Good Nature agents there in order to resist Bad Nature's advances, he occupies the territory. Occupation of the entire yard is the ultimate aim of the yardvolution (semantically, however, occupation suggests an unlawful control of an area, whereas area supremacy suggests legitimate control over an area hard-won through combat).

Execution

A selective killing of a single plant, whether it's a dandelion or a tree, constitutes an execution. Execution is rare in that it typically forms a part of a larger project, e.g. weeding or landscaping.

Sabotage

Sabotage aims to hurt, damage, make useless or destroy vital enemy points, especially roots, in order to prevent further growth. It inflicts a greater degree of destruction than execution. Examples include mulching and selective spraying individual dandelion plants with a strong vinegar solution.

Minuet

The guerrilla yardworker's repertoire should also include minuet. First, he encircles an enemy position in an area of the yard he wishes to transform, e.g. from a dandelion-infested lawn into a reading nook. He begins the fight by removing sod in one corner of the chosen area. He retreats. Bad Nature fights back with grass hanging onto its positions and dandelions coming back up after mere days. The guerrilla initiates a new attack on the lawn in another portion of the projected target area, to which again Bad Nature will respond as before. After removing most of the sod, the guerrilla yardworker returns to finish removing the remaining grass tentacles and dandelions in the areas of the earlier attack.

The movement around the area comes to resemble a dance, with the guerrilla yardworker in constant movement around the area over which he wishes to gain control.

Psychological Operations

The spouse, neighbors, friends, and family aid in the yardvolutionary struggle. Swaying the population to the yardvolution's cause requires psychological operations. From engaging in small talk to conducting more meaningful conversations; from asking for advice to loaning tools; and from sharing the yard's bounty to hosting a garden party, the yardwork guerrilla takes advantage of every opportunity to drum up support or cultivate a positive disposition toward his actions and the yard's transformation. Rarely should the objective of psy-ops be apparent to the target audience, however.

Evasion and Escape

On occasion, the yardwork guerrilla must avoid engaging with enemy forces out in the open. He may determine the time and place are not right and evade Bad Nature's onslaught to focus elsewhere. Escape, by contrast, is a contingency that occurs without warning. When a tree branch or a chimney brick fall, the yardwork guerrilla must act fast to avoid suffering harm.

Alert Shifting

Alert shifting allows the yardwork guerrilla to shuffle among the tactical maneuvers as circumstances command. If he finds himself under attack, he must consider the situation and decide whether to fight in that area. If he determines he cannot fight without getting on the defensive, he must immediately disperse his attention, concentrate on other alternatives, and rapidly shift to another place in the yard where he can fight and emerge victorious. Similar alert shifts can be performed when considering battles along a radius of action where multiple projects are underway. If entering a next phase of an unfinished project threatens to hamper overall progress, the G.Y. must shift to another area or the next, as many times as necessary, until he finds the best place and time to attack.

> "Guerrilla initiative is expressed in dispersion, concentration, and the alert shifting of forces."
> –Mao Tse-Tung

5.3. Follow Up

After achieving the battle objective, the G.Y. tidies the area and retreats. The goal is to leave the target area in the state she wants to find it prior to the next engagement. Whether cleanliness equals godliness remains a matter of dispute, but in the yard it ensures safety, eases future progress, and retains support of the zone's population. Tidying also helps clear the area of obstacles preventing correct situational assessment, re-open any blocked access routes, and organize supplies for easy retrieval. Cleanup makes the yard look good between battles. It is particularly important in multi-phase projects like the brick patio. Any debris or leftover materials must be removed and disposed of in a proper manner. Tools must be returned to the designated storage area. Materials needed for the next phase should be rearranged for visual appeal and easy access.

Because cleanup operations are part of retreat, they immediately follow the successful completion of the attack. The retreat plan outlines the route, manner, and destination of the action. After completing the cleanup, the G.Y. retreats to another area of the yard where she maintains supremacy or to the base. In the former case, she takes up another battle. In the latter, she washes up and resumes her life outside the yard, admiring the results of her work, drawing plans for the next phase, or resting.

5.4. Rest

Following retreat, the G.Y. rests. Periods of rest in-between battles are just as important as the battles themselves. The functions of rest tend to proceed in chronological order and contribute to the cultivation of health (see 5.5.1. Cultivation of Health):

- Give the body a break following intense exertion
- Calm the mind from the stress of combat
- Gather strength for the next engagement

Rest can take as many forms as there are yardwork guerrillas. Most commonly, a shower and a meal immediately follow combat. Stretching exercises, such as yoga, come next. Not to be ignored, stretching aids in the restoration and relaxation of tired muscles. Massage is an excellent technique for kneading tension out of the body, with beneficial medical and relaxation effects. Reading revolutionary literature, interacting with fellow insurgents, or hatching plans for the next mission count as active mental forms of rest. If rest resembles the recharging of batteries, sleep (overnight or nap) remains the principal way to do so.

It is important to differentiate between rest and relaxation. A deliberate action on part of the yardwork guerrilla, rest has a specific purpose: to restore the body and mind to the state prior to battle. Rest fulfills a revolutionary function. By contrast, relaxation lacks deliberation and functionality—it is simply inaction. A truly dedicated yardvolutionary never relaxes because doing so lowers his guard and breeds complacency. Rest reinvigorates the G.Y.; relaxation makes him lazy.

5.5. Activities In-Between Combat Operations

When not resting, the yardwork guerrilla keeps active by preparing for future battles. She can work on cultivating her health, conduct propaganda and recruitment operations (see 3.3.3. Recruitment), or interact with fellow yardvolutionaries.

5.5.1. Cultivation of Health

The only successful yard revolutionary is the one who stays alive and healthy. Self-preservation ranks among the yardwork guerrilla's strategic priorities, but the cultivation of solid health tends to be overlooked. Each G.Y. must, therefore, take care of herself to be battle-ready at any time (see 4.2.4. Preserve Yourself). Exercise, diet and nutrition, and medical care comprise the essential elements of health maintenance.

Exercise

Guerrilla yardwork physically taxes the insurgent enough to question the need for exercise. But the yardvolutionary war generates added demand on her strength, flexibility, and endurance. The strain resulting from guerrilla yardwork requires additional conditioning, balancing, and support. All aerobic exercise grows lung capacity, builds endurance, and relieves built-up stress. Running, especially on hilly trails, reinforces the abdominal core, strengthens legs, and develops quickness. Biking builds lower-body strength and aids the fluidity of movement. Hiking offers the opportunity to walk upright and admire alternate landscapes. Sex offers versatile, vigorous exercise as well, particularly in a time squeeze. It also balances loneliness and helps arouse the spouse's or partner's support for the struggle. Collective sports, such as basketball, soccer, or hockey, too, balance guerrilla yardwork with aerobic exercise, fluidity and range of motion, as well as fellowship.

"At the outset, the essential task of the guerrilla fighter is to keep himself from being destroyed."
–Che Guevara

"Take care of physical health and stay where there are plenty of resources. When there is no sickness in the army, it is said to be invincible. In ancient times skillful warriors first made themselves invincible, and then watched for vulnerability in their opponents."
–Sun Tzu

Exercise allows the yardwork guerrilla to practice self-care away from the yard. Yoga in particular offers multiple benefits:

- Stretching muscles contracted from battle
- Focusing the mind and cultivating mindfulness
- Helping both the body and the mind transition into rest

Endurance builds up due to the yardvolution's long-term character as well as the repetition of various actions during home and yard ownership. Muscle mass builds up over time thanks to the movements guerrilla yardwork requires: digging, hoeing, planting, sowing, weeding, raking, mowing, building, carrying, moving, and even sweeping require omnidirectional movements such as bending, crouching, turning, pushing, pulling, lifting, and others. Guerrilla yardwork is an all-body activity. Unlike exercise done for increasing endurance or building muscle mass, guerrilla yardwork aids both, albeit as an unintentional byproduct of the yardvolutionary change. In fact, it amounts to frequent, if irregular, exercise.

Diet and Nutrition

Early into the yardvolution, a strenuous physical activity, the yardwork guerrilla recognizes that the change in her body's output must be balanced by changes in input. The yard revolution leads to more conscious choices about the food she eats.

Refined, simple carbohydrates, present in products containing refined sugar, high fructose corn syrup (candy, soda), or white flour (bread, pastries), have little to no nutritional value beyond caloric content. Similar to instant gratification from the use of digital technology (see 1.3.3. Reclaim the Self), they provide the guerrilla yardworker's body with a burst of energy that burns quickly and that requires just as rapid replenishment to sustain the effort. In between battles, the G.Y.'s body stores the excess of energy deriving from simple carbs as fat, leading to lethargy and excessive consumption of entertainment media. The danger grows particularly when the revolutionary activity subsides between growing seasons. Processed foods, such as products that come in cans or packages, frozen dinners, or fast food, typically contain higher amounts of sodium, fat, preservatives, and other unhealthy chemicals. Instead, the guerrilla yardworker switches to a balanced diet of whole foods that burn more slowly, helping to sustain her energy for longer periods of time. She aims for her diet to comprise:

- Plenty of fruits and vegetables, many of which she grows in the yard
- Protein, including eggs, lean meat, fish, and legumes
- Complex carbohydrates, such as grains, brown rice, whole wheat, or quinoa
- Limited amount of 'good fats' from items like olive oil and nuts
- Limited amount of dairy, including milk, yogurt, and cheese

Salt helps retain water. In the heat of the growing season, when sustained energy and hydration are paramount, foods with higher salt content can be quite efficient. Items such as bacon, chips-and-salsa, and Chinese food containing soy sauce constitute a solid foundation; salted nuts are an excellent snack; and a salt-rimmed glass of margarita serves well to celebrate a day's accomplishments.

To determine the amount of each element in her diet, the G.Y. seeks guidance from the federal MyPlate program for a balanced diet. She also follows established knowledge and practices regarding nutrition. In any case, if she follows advice presented in this *Handbook*, she becomes attuned to her body so well that she learns to recognize its signals for limiting certain substances and increasing others. In particular, bacon and margaritas can be very addictive, so she takes precautions in their intake. Others, like vegetables, are typically underrepresented on her plate, so she monitors their intake closely. At all times, the G.Y. avoids culinary fads, advice by weight loss gurus, and dieting.

The yard can provide a potentially substantial amount of fruits, vegetables, and herbs (see. 1.3.5. Grow Food, Achieve Self-Sufficiency). Some yardvolutionaries have been known to supply all their vegetables and herbs from the yard during the growing season. As we have seen, eating what the yard provides allows the insurgent to eat healthier and tastier food. The smart G.Y. plants to harvest something throughout the entire growing season, and she plans meals according to what the yard provides. In time, she may find she prefers to eat only the produce the yard yields.

Some 50 to 65 percent of the adult human body comprises water. Hydration is, therefore, a crucial aspect of every guerrilla yardworker's nutrition. One glass of water for every hour worked ought to provide sufficient hydration. A glass of orange juice can supply additional energy before battle. The yardwork guerrilla avoids soda, energy drinks, and flavored water. As a general rule, she also avoids alcohol, especially before and during battle. But, in late afternoon hours, toward the end of battle, or even during breaks in-between easy projects, a beer can lighten the guerrilla yardworker's mood, reprieving her from the stress of the struggle. Many yardwork guerrillas, particularly of Eastern European extraction, also enjoy an occasional shot of spirits—before an attack for courage and afterward to calm the neural tumult.

Medical Care

To avoid injuries or illness, the yardwork guerrilla takes precautions. She wears appropriate clothes and protective equipment (see 5.1.5. Arm Yourself: Yardwork Guerrilla's Equipment). She handles tools, mechanical equipment, and materials according to best practices or instructions. She employs elementary safety measures during combat, e.g. lifting from the crouch not from the bend or placing body parts away from sharp objects such as rotating blades. And she practices a healthy lifestyle.

Preventative measures help avoid the need for medical care. However, the prudent yardwork guerrilla is prepared, with supplies and skills, to self-administer basic first aid for non-life threatening scrapes, cuts, punctures, wounds, or other injuries. For extreme cases she has a contingency plan in place to receive medical advice over the phone or seek care at the nearest medical facility.

5.5.2. Propaganda

Guerrilla yardwork extends beyond the yard; a philosophy and a method, it must be spread to maximum possible extent. Propaganda disseminates the messages of guerrilla yardwork, publicizes its successes; persuades the zone's population; and sways neighbors to its path (see 3.3.3. Recruitment).

Every active G.Y. has the responsibility to conduct propaganda operations. First he must determine his objective. Is he merely showcasing his prowess in the yard? Is he highlighting how he executed a particular project? Providing advice on a specific tactic? Is he attempting to recruit additional insurgents?

Next he must decide on his target audience. Neighbors, family, friends, coworkers, acquaintances and others can provide easy targets for propaganda efforts. The yardwork guerrilla must then decide on the message. Too often an overt pitch accomplishes the opposite of the intended goal. Best to simply highlight one's successes and recommend ways to emulate them.

Finally, the G.Y. must determine the best channels to share the selected message. The main media of guerrilla yardwork propaganda include:

- *Conversation.* Verbal communication can often achieve more than other means. Particularly

> "The guerrilla fighter as a social reformer should not only provide an example in his own life but he ought also constantly to give orientation in ideological problems, explaining what he knows and what he wishes to do at the right time. One of the characteristics of revolutionary propaganda must be truth. The revolutionary idea should be diffused by means of appropriate media to the greatest depth possible. Little by little, in this way, the masses will be won over."
> –Che Guevara

in informal settings, like parties, a conversation struck with a friend or newly introduced stranger can lead to a successful conversion. Home and yard ownership provides excellent fodder for small talk, which can then grow into the discussion of guerrilla yardwork. Because the *Handbook* opens the door to discussing guerrilla yardwork, an alternative is to mention having recently read it and then recommend it.

- *Meetup.* The G.Y. can organize or join a gathering of people interested in gardening and share his messages there. But because overt sales efforts can backfire, he must never hijack the conversation and push the issue. Carrying a copy of the *Handbook* or wearing a Guerrilla Yardwork T-shirt at these events can spark conversations as well.

- *Leaflets, pamphlets, brochures, and other print collateral.* The yardwork guerrilla can distribute printed materials containing the method's main tenets and references to further resources. He can hand them out, post them on notice boards, or leave them behind at appropriate places (taking care, of course, not to litter). He can easily create the needed materials using lines from this *Handbook*, with appropriate attribution.

- *T-shirts, sweatshirts, mugs, and other branded items.* Displaying the yardvolution messages on various items embeds them in people's minds and starts conversations. The power rests in numbers—the more merchandise is out there, visible to the masses, the better the exposure (it may take up to 9 times to hear a message in order to remember it). The G.Y. wears his colors proudly.

- *Social media.* The GuerrillaYardwork.com website and Guerrilla Yardwork Facebook page are the main online hubs of guerrilla yardwork. There the G.Y. obtains more information; relays his successes by publishing guest blog posts, blog comments, and Facebook updates; shares photos and videos about his projects; grabs and shares links and embeddable code

snippets; and sends messages directly to his contacts. Finally, Pinning, Digging, Weeding and using any other social media platform he likes extends the message to additional online circles. Writing a blog about his yardvolution takes content creation to the next level and cannot be recommended enough.

- *Traditional media.* Local newspapers or websites often feature articles or columns about gardening. The yardwork guerrilla should contact their authors or editors to suggest stories.

5.5.3. Communication and Social Networking

Though the yardwork guerrilla carries out her duties by herself, she is no island; communication is an important aspect of her struggle. She must communicate with her family in the base and all neighbors to cultivate their support. She must also interact with fellow yardvolutionaries (see 3.3. The Yardvolutionary Army).

Communication tools in the G.Y.'s arsenal are as diverse as humanity itself. The most popular channels include:

- Verbal conversation in all its tonal variety
- Exclamations and laughter
- Gestures
- Phone
- Regular or 'snail' mail
- Email

Alternative methods, such as two cans linked with string, smoke signals, and sun-reflecting mirrors work as well, albeit with coding and decoding challenges. Carrier pigeons carry the burden of housing and diseases. Uninformed guerrilla yardworkers can easily mistake carrier pigeons for pests and murder them.

"It is necessary to maintain stable lines of communication."
– Che Guevara

Social media tools open a myriad of possibilities to microbroadcast to friendly masses and to communicate directly with other individuals. Wherever the G.Y. has a presence in the social media landscape, she should take every opportunity to share the yardvolution's message. She posts progress updates, including photos and videos, about her yard projects; asks for advice on the use or sourcing of tools and materials; shares links to guerrilla yardwork-related resources; re-posts (re-tweets, re-blogs, shares, etc.) other insurgents' updates and links; and caps it all with inspirational quotes from this *Handbook*.

5.6. The Seven Sins of the Yardwork Guerrilla

Preparation and prevention are the hallmarks of the successful guerrilla yardworker and the prerequisites to victory. No matter how much he plans or prepares, errors creep into his conduct in the course of a long war. Hence he must study the most frequent missteps that guerrilla yardworkers commit and avoid repeating them.

1. *Inexperience.* High atop the food chain, the yardwork guerrilla may view Bad Nature as stupid and believe victories come easy. Or he may think a complete yard transformation is impossible and the yardvolutionary war endless. In both cases, failure is assured. Only with

experience gained in the course of combat can the G.Y. correctly estimate his and the adversary's forces and gain confidence in his success. The greenhorn yardwork guerrilla first undertakes simple projects. With each engagement he gathers courage and audacity that propel him to the next battle and the next.

2. *Boasting.* The G.Y. may be tempted to broadcast his battle victories high and wide, drawing unnecessary attention to himself and his struggle. Manifestations of this sin include talking about his projects with friends or neighbors without prompting, pointing out the new features of the front yard to passersby, or making announcements from the roof of his house with a megaphone. The prudent guerrilla yardworker assesses the course of each battle, draws up a brief report, and shares his findings with fellow insurgents through proper channels.

"Even when the guerrilla applies his revolutionary technique with precision and rigorously abides by security rules, he can still be vulnerable to errors. There is no perfect guerrilla. One of the methods to diminish the margin of error is to know thoroughly the seven sins of the guerrilla and try to fight them."
–Carlos Marighella, re-interpreted

3. *Vanity.* Blinded by success, the guerrilla yardworker may see himself as the center of the universe. The humble G.Y. recognizes his place in the world and the interconnection of all things. He knows that both he and his yardvolution occupy but a tiny part of history and that on the grand scale of the universe they are more insignificant than a deer turd in a lavender patch.

4. *Exaggeration.* If vanity goes unchecked, the G.Y. may exaggerate his strength and think of himself as invulner-

able and unbeatable. Such an insurgent may undertake projects for which he lacks forces, skill, or equipment, exposing himself to harm or failure. Other manifestations of this sin include chest beating, fist pumping, and failing to take basic safety precautions. The aware G.Y. recognizes his limits and approaches the yardvolution with calm and resolve—hallmarks of a realistic outlook.

5. *Precipitous action.* Sometimes the desire to complete a project can overwhelm the yardwork guerrilla so much that he throws himself into action without proper preparation. But, as we have seen, thorough preparation ought to precede every battle. The successful G.Y. arms himself with patience and takes all the steps necessary to ensure a victorious battle.

6. *Anger.* It is easy to lose one's marbles in the course of guerrilla yardwork: a project is taking too long to complete; dandelions, presumed exterminated, return to infest the lawn; squirrels procreate to no end. Though a small dose of anger is hard to avoid and can, in fact, fuel motivation, anger ought not to drive the yardvolution because it blinds the guerrilla. The G.Y. should let the temper die down before an attack.

7. *Failure to plan.* An attack of the nerves, whether from the loss of patience or out of anger, sometimes causes the G.Y. to lose patience and forgo planning. While improvisation belongs to his arsenal, a solid plan must underpin it—there must be something to diverge from in order to diverge. The yardwork guerrilla plans the war, every attack, and every phase of every project to achieve victory in the yardvolutionary war.

.

Acknowledgments

Guerrilla yardwork owes its greatest debt to those who fought their yardvolution without knowing it. Foremost among them is my father, *Michal Korchňak*. After a full week's, mostly manual, work at the railway, he would spend his weekends working in the yard at the family cabin alongside my mother (though he'd do the heavy lifting)—they both would call laboring at the cabin the best way to relax. Once he built an electric lawn mower from parts in the cabin's shop. The grass didn't know what hit it. His eventual return to the scythe due to its superior handling and grass cutting inspired my appreciation for age-old, human-powered tools. I hated life (and him) when he had me carry buckets full of rocks from the creek at the bottom of the hill on which the cabin sat up to the top of the property where we were building a foundation for an extension. But the work got done, I got some muscles out of it, and there's a story to tell.

I am also thankful to

- *Mike Russell*, an incipient first-time home and yard owner and editor par excellence, for reviewing an early draft of the *Handbook* and sharing constructive suggestions. Find Mike at PivotalWriting.com.
- *Frank Sharpy* for teaching me the one rule of landscaping: "Green side up."

- *Volker Busse* for the beautiful free fonts.
- *Susan Bender Phelps* and *Mazarine Treyz* for their in-person and *Ariel Gore* for her book's mentorship, encouragement, and marketing advice.
- *Lindsay Sauvé* for endless encouragement, moral support, reading and re-reading of early drafts, and, of course, guerrilla yardworking with me.

Finally, thank *you*, dear yardwork guerrilla—because you are one, right?—for reading this *Handbook*. May it provide bushels of inspiration for your journey through your own private yardvolution. Please share your experience, through comments, photos, or videos, at GuerrillaYardwork.com or on the book's Facebook page at Facebook.com/GuerrillaYardwork. And if you know a fellow home and yard owner who might find this book useful, buy them their own copy. They're going to need all the help they can get.

Sources and Inspiration

Guerrilla Yardwork is a field manual that presents an alternative understanding and practice of yardwork. Every section can branch out into a small library. Many books, magazines, and websites provide specific gardening advice and refer to further reading. The list below contains all the books and articles used in the writing of the *Handbook*. Years in parentheses show the original year of publication, if known. All short URL's are case-sensitive and functional as of publication date, but should any of them malfunction, the guerrilla reader can find the full links at GuerrillaYardwork.com/Sources. In addition, *Wikipedia* opened doors to many topics. Finally, all "Buy at..." links are affiliate links as part of American Robotnik's participation in the Amazon Associates program. Every purchase you make of a book on the list below covers the cost of one cup of coffee I drank every weekday morning between January and July 2012, from 5:45 a.m. to 7 a.m., to fuel the writing of this book before commuting to my day job. More importantly, your purchase also supports the authors who put their own blood, sweat, tears, and caffeine into their creations. Thank you.

American Horticultural Society. "AHS Heat-Zone Map." Retrieved from http://bit.ly/NGDmaG on 7/21/2012.

Brenzel, Kathleen Norris, ed. *Sunset Western Garden Book*. Menlo Park, CA: Sunset Publishing, 2001. Buy at http://amzn.to/I8UNKm.

Chalquist, Craig. "What is Terrapsychology?" Retrieved from http://www.terrapsych/whatisTP.html on 4/2/2012.

Crawford, Matthew "Shop Class as Soulcraft." *New Atlantis*, 2006. Retrieved from http://bit.ly/HoYize on 3/21/2012.

Csikszentmihalyi, Mihalyi. *Flow: The Psychology of Optimal Experience*. New York: Harper Perennial, 2008 (1990). Buy at http://amzn.to/I8V2Fg.

De Groot, Rodney et al. "Protecting Wood Fences for Yard and Garden." University of Wisconsin-Extension/Madison, 1979. Retrieved from http://bit.ly/HV0wo8 on 3/22/2012.

Duany, Andres, Elizabeth Plater-Zyberk, and Jeff Speck. *Suburban Nation: The Rise of Sprawl and the Decline of the American Dream*. New York: North Point Press, 2010 (2000). Buy at http://amzn.to/OkSw5s.

Emerson, Ralph Waldo. "Self-Reliance." In: *Essays*. 1841. Retrieved from http://bit.ly/L8n44C on 5/10/2012.

Firefly, Rufus and Mike Benton. *White Trash Gardening*. Taylor Pub, 1996. Buy at http://amzn.to/NtMxX5.

Guevara, Che. *Guerrilla Warfare*. Lincoln, Nebraska: University of Nebraska Press, 1998 (1960/1963). Buy at http://amzn.to/I8VFPl.

Hart, Rhonda Massingham. *Dirt Cheap Gardening: Hundreds of Ways to Save Money in Your Garden*. North Adams, MA: Storey Publishing, 1995. Buy at http://amzn.to/NtOV01.

HGTV.com. "Designer's Portfolio: Outdoor Living Spaces." Retrieved from http://bit.ly/PauaMZ on 7/4/2012.

"Interview with Marshal McLuhan." *Wired*, Issue 4.01, January 1996. Retrieved from http://bit.ly/HoZ4ME on 3/22/2012.

Johnson, Lorraine. *City Farmer: Adventures in Urban Food Growing*. Vancouver: Greystone Books, 2010. Buy at http://amzn.to/NtNuPp.

Kilcullen, David. "Counterinsurgency Redux." *Survival*, Vol. 48, No. 4 (2006). Retrieved from http://bit.ly/HoTrOr on 4/5/2012.

Kirn, Walter Kirn. "The Autumn of the Multitaskers." *The Atlantic*, November 2007. Retrieved from http://bit.ly/Hp0eb1 on 3/22/2012.

Lanier, Jaron. *You Are Not a Gadget: A Manifesto*. New York: Alfred A. Knopf, 2010. Buy at http://amzn.to/NtNJK4.

Lao Tsu. *Tao Te Ching*. Translated by Gia-Fu Feng and Jane English. New York: Vintage Books, 1989. Buy at http://amzn.to/NtNYF9.

Lenin, Vladimir Ilyich. "Guerrilla Warfare." *Proletary* No. 5 (1906), in *Lenin Collected Works*, Vol. 11, pp. 213-223. Moscow: Progress Publishers, 1965. Retrieved from Marxists Internet Archive, http://bit.ly/I7al4P, on 4/6/2012.

Löw, Martina. "The Constitution of Space: The Structuration of Spaces Through the Simultaneity of Effect and Perception." *European Journal of Social Theory*, Vol. 11, No. 1 (2008): 25-49.

Mao Tse-Tung. *On Guerrilla Warfare*. Translated by Brig. Gen. Samuel B. Griffith, USMC (Ret.). New York: Praeger Publishers, 1961. (1937). Buy at http://amzn.to/I8VW4I.

Marighella, Carlos. *Mini-Manual of the Urban Guerrilla*. 1969. Retrieved from http://bit.ly/Lvk7BH.

Mazur, Christopher and Ellen Wilson. "2010 Census Brief: Housing Characteristics 2010." Washington, D.C.: United States Census Bureau, October 2011.

McKay, George. *Radical Gardening: Politics, Idealism & Rebellion in the Garden*. London: Frances Lincoln Limited, 2011. Buy at http://amzn.to/NtOdzX.

Mokyr, Joel. *The Lever of Riches: Technological Creativity and Economic Progress*. New York: Oxford University Press, 1990. Buy at http://amzn.to/IjVwwG.

National Association of Realtors. "NAR Home Buyer and Seller Survey Reflects Tight Credit Conditions." Press Release. Anaheim: November 11, 2011. Retrieved from http://bit.ly/JTlgT6 on 5/16/2012.

Pallenberg, Barbara. *Guerrilla Gardening: How to Create Gorgeous Gardens for Free.* Los Angeles: Renaissance Books, 2001. Buy at http://amzn.to/NtNjTZ.

Pierce, Charles. "The First 3,650 Days." *Esquire,* January 2010. Retrieved from http://bit.ly/KYM6ZI on 6/15/2012.

Pope, Alexander. "Epistle IV to Richard Boyle, Earl of Burlington of the Use of Riches." In: *The Complete Poetical Works of Alexander Pope.* Cambridge Edition, ed. Henry W. Boynton. Boston and New York: Houghton, Mifflin and Co., 1903 (1708-1712). Retrieved from *Wikipedia* and http://bit.ly/HUWXyc on 4/5/2012.

Rao, Venkatesh. "A Brief History of the Corporation: 1600 to 2100." *Ribbon Farm,* June 8, 2011. Retrieved from http://bit.ly/Hp0DtU on 3/23/2012.

Reynolds, Richard. *On Guerrilla Gardening: A Handbook for Gardening Without Boundaries.* New York: Bloomsbury USA, 2008. Buy at http://amzn.to/I8W3x7.

Russell, Betrand. "In Praise of Idleness." 1932. Retrieved from http://bit.ly/HoUlKM on 4/5/2012.

Shields, David. *Reality Hunger: A Manifesto.* New York: Vintage, 2011. Buy at http://amzn.to/P9Jg5t.

Simmel, Georg. "The Metropolis and Mental Life." 1903. Retrieved from http://bit.ly/HoUs9o on 3/19/2012.

Sun Tzu. *The Art of War.* Translated by Thomas Cleary. Boston: Shambala, 2005. (Approx. 6th century BCE - 12th century CE). Buy at http://amzn.to/I8WCan.

Swerdlow, Joel. *Nature's Medicine: Plants That Heal.* Washington, DC: National Geographic Society, 2000. Buy at http://amzn.to/PaBCrz.

Teaford, Jon. *The American Suburb: The Basics.* New York: Routledge, 2007. Buy at http://amzn.to/OkSSJi.

Tillotson, Betty, ed. *Skills for Simple Living.* Point Roberts, WA: The Smallholder Publishing Collective, 1991. Buy at http://amzn.to/LWClg5.

Tracey, David. *Guerrilla Gardening: A Manualfesto.* Gabriola Island, BC: New Society Publishers, 2007. Buy at http://amzn.to/NtLYNc.

—————. *Urban Agriculture: Ideas and Designs for the New Food Revolution.* Gabriola Island, BC: New Society Publishers, 2011. Buy at http://amzn.to/TekRIV.

Turkle, Sherry. *Alone Together: Why We Expect More from Technology and Less from Each Other.* New York: Basic Books, 2011. Buy at http://amzn.to/L8nB6H.

United States Department of Agriculture. "Let's Eat for the Health of It: A Dietary Guidelines Consumer Brochure." Retrieved from http://1.usa.gov/P9Kjm7 on 7/4/2012.

—————. "USDA Plant Hardiness Zone Map." Retrieved from http://1.usa.gov/NGDoPY on 7/21/2012.

United States Department of the Army. *U.S. Army Guerrilla Warfare Handbook.* New York: Skyhorse Publishing, 2009. Buy at http://amzn.to/I8V9ka.

United States Department of Defense. *Dictionary of Military and Associated Terms.* Joint Publication 1-02, 8 November 2010, as amended through 15 February 2012. Retrieved from http://1.usa.gov/I8TXNO on 3/22/2012.

Vlad, Liviu Bogdan. "Urban Aesthetics: Emergence and Development." *Theoretical and Empirical Researches in Urban Management*, Vol. 3, No. 12 (2009). Retrieved from http://bit.ly/I7aNA4 on 3/23/2012.

"Your Yard: A User's Manual." *Esquire*, May 2012, pp. 78-81.

"A yard can be a pain
in the ass."
-*Esquire*